Captaincy

Also in the Sporting Skills series

PACE BOWLING Bob Willis
WICKETKEEPING Bob Taylor
THE ALL-ROUNDER Peter Walker
SPIN BOWLING Ray Illingworth
BATTING Graham Gooch

SPORTING SKILLS SERIES

Captaincy

RAY ILLINGWORTH

WITH THE ASSISTANCE OF MIKE CALVIN
(REG HAYTER LTD)

PELHAM BOOKS

First published in Great Britain by
PELHAM BOOKS LTD
44 Bedford Square
London WC1B 3DU
1980

The photographs are reproduced by courtesy of the following (the numbers refer to the pages on which the photographs fall): Adrian Murrell, Allsport, 22, 42 (below), 45, 74, 89, 93, 95; Central Press Photos Ltd, 17, 25, 41, 72, 82, 97, (left), 99, 101, 113; Colorsport, 62; Patrick Eagar, 10, 21, 40, 47, 56, 69, 87, 97 (right), 103, 107, 109, 115, 117; Ken Kelly, 15, 50-1, 105, 111; Press Association Ltd, 28, 42 (above); Sport and General, 80; Sporting Pictures (UK) Ltd, 34-5; Bob Thomas, 38

ISBN 0 7207 1262 9

Typeset by Cambrian Typesetters, Farnborough, Hampshire
Printed in Great Britain by Hollen Street Press, Slough
and bound by Dorstel Press Ltd, Harlow

Contents

1 A Man for all Seasons 7
2 How to Select a Captain 14
3 Elementary... 24
4 Look and Learn 37
5 In the Field 53
6 Man Management 65
7 The Pressures of Today 77
8 Captains I Have Known 86

1 A Man for all Seasons

One word sums up a successful cricket captain: versatile. He needs the patience of a saint, the diplomacy of an ambassador, the compassion of a social worker and the skin of a rhino. Boundless enthusiasm, the insight of a psychologist and the smooth-talking style of a con-man might also come in handy.

Clearly, there is more to being a captain than having an asterisk by your name in the scorebook. You have to be the proverbial jack-of-all-trades and, hopefully, master of some. But do not abandon your ambitions in the mistaken belief that such a person is born and not made. At whatever level you play, the natural gift of leadership has to be complemented by technical knowledge that can only be gained through dedication and a genuine love of cricket.

The hallmark of a potential captain is that he is always willing to listen and learn. I am sure, for instance, that Donald Waterhouse and Harry Bailes, two distinguished former Bradford League cricketers, did not realize they were shaping a future England skipper as they rolled the wicket at Farsley cricket club.

I was a shy youngster who gladly helped the pair every Tuesday and Thursday. The square was flooded early in the week, and while we rolled the pitch in preparation for the weekend we would talk animatedly about the game. I have enjoyed a long career in first-class cricket since those idyllic evenings, but the things I learned and the attitudes expressed have never been forgotten.

I admit I was lucky to be brought up in the Pudsey/Farsley

area, which nestles between Bradford and Leeds. It was cricket's equivalent of being born with a silver spoon in my mouth. Although small compared with the large industrial conurbations nearby – before the war the population was less than 10,000 – the district has an astonishing cricket tradition. It is steeped in the game, and has produced many outstanding players.

When I first played for Yorkshire in 1951 I was one of four members of the team who had been born in Pudsey. At the time the county had not been without a Pudsey player since the 1890s, and we were acutely aware of carrying on the tradition. Greats like Herbert Sutcliffe and Sir Len Hutton spent some of their careers in local cricket.

But it is not essential that a captain should come from one of cricket's hotbeds. What you must have, whether your stage be the village green or a Test arena, is common sense. Problems should be thought over logically, both on and off the field. It is no good having a skipper who is prone to panic under pressure. A cool temperament is vital, especially with the growing domination of limited-overs cricket, which demands instant decisions and a clear appreciation of all the possibilities. If the captain is seen not to be in control of the situation, his team will degenerate into a disorganized outfit incapable of living up to its potential.

That is just one aspect of the psychological side of captaincy, which goes hand in hand with the practical part of the job. A good captain is a good judge of character. He needs to know how to get the best out of his players – and how to exploit the fallibilities of his opponents. The ability to read batsmen is built up over the years. Once you recognize a failing, never forget it. One useful tip in assessing a batsman's strengths and weaknesses is to notice how he holds the bat. A batsman involuntarily betrays his favourite shots by his grip.

The captain is involved in a sustained cat-and-mouse game with the batsman. As in any battle there are valid tactical reaons for attack and retreat. Never be afraid to attack the strengths of the man at the crease. You can lure a batsman into throwing his wicket away by stealthily setting a trap and then feeding a favourite shot, such as the hook.

Similarly, you must remember that your own team has its peculiar human foibles and failings. Your men are not robots. They react in different ways in the same situation and respond to different treatment by the captain. Some give their best after being hurt by forcibly expressed criticism. For example, Tony Lock, the former Surrey and England spinner, would give extra effort after being cursed by his captain. However, while you can nag the best out of some players, others need gentle encouragement. Geoff Boycott, for instance, constantly needs reassuring how good a batsman he is. Insecurity? Maybe, but it is your job as a captain to capitalize on failings like that for the good of the team.

A captain, having succeeded by various methods in inspiring his team towards a common objective, must know how to use their enthusiasm. It is imperative that he can read a wicket and know when to utilize certain types of bowlers. It is worthless having speed, swing and spin specialists unless they are used at the right time. Having said that, it must be realized that reading a wicket is no easy task. Even vastly experienced internationals make damaging decisions that can cost a Test match. A captain must learn to trust his intuition, and attempt to gain as much local knowledge as possible.

It is difficult to say conclusively what is the ideal temperament for a captain. I firmly believe, however, that the extrovert will always have an advantage over the introvert. That is because the captain of any sporting team is a social animal. He must be able to mix comfortably with his side.

I feel it is important for a captain to be 'one of the lads' in a social sense. I certainly do not advocate the skipper drinking to excess with his team, but he should make an effort to mingle in a relaxed environment with them. The natural loner finds this extremely hard, and does not have the personality that can sometimes act as a catalyst for greater effort on the field. Of course, there are exceptions that prove every rule. Sir Len Hutton,

aloof and somewhat uneasy in company, got by as a captain because of his experience and the respect of his batting ability engendered in his players.

One does not have to have an enormous amount of day-to-day experience in county cricket before taking over as captain. Two years as a regular at first-class cricket level is all the preparation required to be a county captain, especially if there is not an illustrious record of success to live up to.

Attitude is more important than experience. Therefore, ten years' hard labour on the county circuit should never be a prerequisite for a Test captain. What is essential is a thoughtful, committed approach to cricket. Those players who are quite happy to drift down to third man and never give the game another thought, save for their personal contribution, will struggle with the responsibilities of captaincy. A captain does not think for one, but eleven. A single moment's blissful lack of concentration can be costly.

All sorts of things can go wrong if slackness is allowed to creep in. Field placings have to be watched, bowlers advised, batsmen analysed and, in the case of limited-overs cricket, run rates calculated. Only the responsible, thinking cricketer could cope with such pressure. Be it at club or international level, I believe a person with such qualities needs a maximum of ten games in charge to get used to handling players and making snap decisions.

I would have no hesitation in aligning myself with the ranks of responsible players. Even as a lad in short pants, when I rode around Bradford on my bicycle intent on cheering Len Hutton to as many runs as possible, I used to be a keen student of the tactical side of the game. I listened, looked and learned. That was recognized by my school, who made me cricket captain. I went on to lead Farsley Juniors, and, at the tender age of 17, occasionally captained the senior side in the Bradford League. Being in charge of a team that included professionals old enough to be my father proved a significant part of my cricketing education.

After army service I graduated to the Yorkshire playing staff.

OPPOSITE, *Geoff Boycott at his happiest – at the crease*

Ronnie Burnet, who led the team in 1958 and 1959, had a profound impression on my thinking. Ronnie, the very opposite of a big-name captain, was 39 when he took over, an amateur who inherited a side that had previously included too many dressing-room lawyers and not enough positive leadership. Without him, Yorkshire could not have enjoyed their glorious run of success that included seven County Championships between 1959 and 1968. He rebuilt team spirit by being honest with his players, each one of whom was treated fairly.

I benefitted from that refreshing policy when Ken Taylor, an undeniably talented opening batsman who also played soccer for Huddersfield Town, wanted one of his periodic moves down the order. Previously, he had been allowed to change at will and soon after Ronnie took over he expressed a desire to bat at number five, where I was playing with great success and confidence. If I had been sacrificed to his whims it would have been a bitter blow, and Ronnie realized this. Despite the fact that he had come through the ranks with Taylor, he insisted that he should go in at number six for the first time in his career. I appreciated that piece of shrewd captaincy, and repaid him by making five hundreds in the latter half of the 1959 season.

Ronnie's recognition of the importance of confidence to any player also helped Doug Padgett, a lifetime friend and current Yorkshire coach. A prodigy who made his county debut at 16, 'Padge' was a wholehearted player who was held back by his lack of belief in himself. Ronnie was quick to spot this, so before the start of the 1959 season he took Padge to one side and said: 'Forget about worrying. I guarantee you a place at number three in the order this season. All I want is you to justify that faith by scoring runs.' Doug duly obliged, totalling 2,181 runs in his best summer. Some might say that Ronnie took a reckless risk by pledging Padge a regular place, but I saw it as a marvellous example of a captain knowing and trusting his players. He knew Padge was a conscientious batsman who had not been encouraged in the right way, and was prepared to give him a chance.

A good captain is never afraid to ask advice from his players, but one can have too much of a good thing. This was recognized by Vic Wilson, the successor to Ronnie Burnet, when he was trying to nurture the delicate talents of Don Wilson. Slow left-armer Don, now MCC head coach, was an ebullient ever-optimistic bowler, but deep down was a little insecure. He was especially prone to confusion when confronted by varying opinions within the side about his style and action. Vic realized this, and, keen to protect his bowler, decreed that only myself, at the time the most experienced spinner in the team, was allowed to give Don any coaching. I was heartened by the captain's gesture, and did my best to help a team-mate fulfil his undoubted potential.

My early days at Yorkshire rammed home the message that all players, regardless of experience and reputation, must be expected to observe the same rules. Standards of dress, discipline and punctuality should apply to everyone from the raw recruit to the Test star. Nothing is more damaging to team spirit than if a weak captain allows a privileged few senior professionals to do virtually as they please. A captain can by all means give the more established player a little leeway. But first such a player must earn it by showing a responsible attitude that illustrates that he will not betray his skipper's trust.

I make a point of stressing to any would-be captain that he must expect to be all things to all men. It is a personal job which no two cricketers do alike. But the satisfaction when your team puts all the theory and planning into practice is enormous.

2 How to Select a Captain

Mike Brearley was not allowed the personal, private anguish endured by every batsman when the runs dry up. He was in the exposed position of England captain, and his struggle for form attracted critics all too eager to remind him of his failings. I felt deeply for Brearley. The pressure to submit to the jibes that he was not good enough as a batsman to warrant a place in international cricket must have been great.

Brearley's situation brought into the open the age-old dilemma of whether a captain should be worth his place in the side. There are two options available. You can either build a team around a natural leader or pick the captain from the best eleven players around.

I believe that at county and Test level a captain needs to have the basic talent to justify him occupying a valuable place in the team. But at club level the circumstances are significantly different. A club captain does not need to be one of the better players. A born leader who can inspire others by his firmness, ability to take criticism and general will-to-win is the ideal choice. Such a person is well equipped to encourage and enthuse young players, which is his most important job. A youngster, fresh from school and eager to learn, may well be put off by a captain who places an intolerable importance on results and his own form.

In the hard-nosed world of professional cricket a captain must have the talent to go with the ability to inspire. Yet before a skipper is chosen it is important to define what is meant by

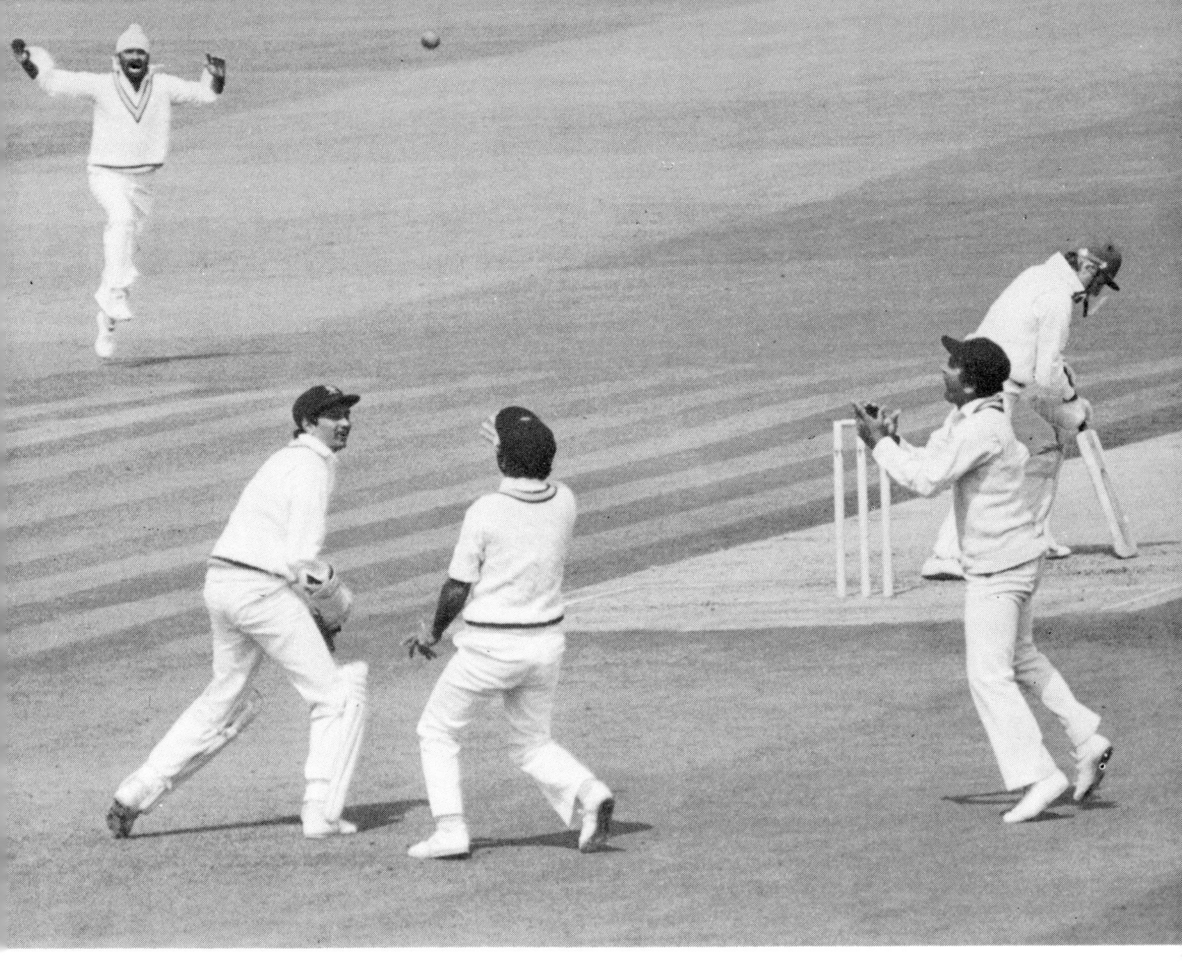

Brearley's struggle for form continues as the Indian fielders celebrate his wicket

'being worth a place in the side'. It must be remembered that a good leader of men can contribute something to the side. A great bowler or batsman may have the potential to destroy opponents, but shrewd captaincy can have the same effect. A captain does not have to average 100 with the bat. A man who handles people well and has the knack of reading a game quickly and accurately can be equally valuable, even if he averages little more than 20.

That said, at the highest echelons of the game the requirements are more stringent. I have to admit that, despite my sympathy, England are a less potent batting side with Brearley in the line-up.

I assumed the England captaincy in 1969 when the selectors used the traditional Australian method of picking their leader. They chose what they considered to be the best eleven players in the country, and appointed me as captain from that group. That is the best policy when there is no outstanding leader in the country. I would, however, condone picking a brilliant captain not quite worth his place on natural ability alone. If you appoint a man who can drag 110 per cent out of the team by his personality, he is worth an extra half a player.

The path to success is made smoother if the captain has done some bowling. By that I do not mean he should wheel away for 1,000 overs a summer, but it is invaluable if he knows from experience the problems a bowler can suffer. You might not believe it, but even the speed merchants who charge in, bull-like, from near the boundary rail are sensitive souls, prone to frustration and self doubt. If a captain is solely a batsman there is a danger that he will fail to understand the difficulties of men who can win a match for him.

My career as a captain was undoubtedly aided by the fact that I was a bowler. I was able to recognize the trials and tribulations my bowlers were going through, and tried to help them with advice and unobtrusive encouragement. In many cases, because of my background of bowling on different wickets in varying circumstances, I could literally read my bowlers' minds. That has to help.

It would be difficult to over-emphasize the importance of having a cohesive policy of attack when you are in the field. If you lose control of your opponent's innings, you lose the game.

There is little a captain can do when his side is batting. He is not totally helpless – it is essential he talks to a batsman before he goes in to bat – but he has no influence once his men are at the crease. In contrast, you are in control of your team's destiny when in the field. Bowlers can, and should, be helped all the time.

Having a specialist batsman, especially an opener, as captain can bring problems. Through no fault of their own batsmen as a breed have little understanding of bowlers. Most seem to believe

Richie Benaud – a brilliant captain

that bowling is relatively simple and do not realize the mental effect a dropped catch or a slack piece of fielding can have. Batsmen's eternal search for runs can also get on top of them. John Whitehouse, for instance, resigned as Warwickshire captain in autumn 1979, citing the responsibilities of leading the team for his lack of form with the bat. If a batsman/captain is struggling for personal success it is inevitable his mind will occasionally wander from the task in hand. The most common time is when the bowlers are trying to wheedle out the last pair. It is all too easy for a captain to begin the mental preparations for his next innings when there is a job still to be done in the field.

I find it telling that international captains like myself, Richie Benaud, Gary Sobers and Tony Greig were all-rounders. Our common denominator was that we understood both bowlers and batsmen, which made it easier for us to lead the side effectively.

A person who bats in the middle order and plays a supporting role as a bowler – proof of his versatility – makes the best captain. And of all the great captains who have emerged from the all rounders' category none has been greater than Benaud. He won the Ashes in 1961 on his only tour of England as captain. That is testament enough to his ability, because Australia were the underdogs against an England side that had a good depth of batting and a potent bowling attack spearheaded by Fred Trueman and Brian Statham.

My first-hand knowledge of his ability to coax the best out of his players is restricted to six weeks playing under him for a Commonwealth team that toured South Africa in 1961. The relentless march of time since then has done nothing to dim the immense impact he had on me.

I remain convinced I would have been a twenty per cent better bowler if Benaud had captained me regularly for a season or two. He had an infectious enthusiasm and knew the mentality of bowlers, who can be pessimistic and lack a little confidence. If I didn't think I was going to take a wicket, Richie would soon convince me otherwise. He was willing to attack sensibly and help the bowler by putting on pressure at the right time.

A specialist bowler can suffer from being saddled with the responsibilities of leadership. Like the opening batsman, he can worry about his personal contribution. There is also the danger of pandering to the cynics. He can find himself in a Catch 22 situation. If the wickets are good he can be accused of under-bowling himself, and if he cleans up the tailenders he leaves himself open to petty claims that he is using his position as captain to capture easy wickets.

If a bowler is to be captain he must have a strong character – like Stuart Surridge, who was at the helm when Surrey began their run of seven successive Championships in the 1950s. Stuart was larger than life. Commanding on the field, he was a playful, mischievous man off it. It would have been fitting if his middle name was confidence, because his unique pre-play predictions were an entertaining feature of our visits to The Oval.

As an amateur he used to change in a separate room from his team, which was situated next to the visitors' dressing room. When we were changing we would often hear a knock on the door and be serenaded by Stuart's gravelly voice forecasting: 'It has rained just enough for you, Yorkshire. You won't last above two hours out there this morning.'

Worcestershire found out these were no idle boasts in 1954. Put into bat on the first day after rain had delayed the start until 2 pm, they were all out for 25. Surridge, full of optimism as usual, then declared Surrey's innings at 92-3. His calculated gamble came off when Worcestershire were dismissed for 40 by 12.30 the next day. Surridge's confidence in his team had earned a victory by an innings and 27 runs in less than a day's playing time.

Theoretically, the wicketkeeper is best suited to captaincy. The nature of his job demands commitment and concentration, two essential qualities in any leader of men. He has to set an example in the field, is involved in every delivery and is in the best position to assess what impact individual bowlers are having.

However, in practice the added responsibility of decision-making tends to prove too much. Nevertheless, a captain can still utilize the advantages a wicketkeeper has, and that means turning to him for advice. I made a point of consulting with Alan Knott when I captained England. He was alert, read the game well, and was eager to help. He could see more from behind the stumps than I could from my accustomed position at gully, and gave invaluable information which I used in planning bowling changes and tactical switches.

Men like Knott have a gruelling job and it is significant that no wicketkeeper has made a real impact as a captain. Bob Taylor has a great store of knowledge, but was not a success when he answered a familiar Derbyshire crisis by taking over as county captain in the middle of the 1975 season. 'Chat' is a conscientious man, but lasted less than a year in the job, mainly because he was reluctant to take the unpleasant disciplinary decisions that have to be made by any skipper.

Of all the current wicketkeepers David Bairstow of Yorkshire has the best chance of developing into a solid county captain. He is an affable extrovert whose brash exterior belies the serious way he studies the game. I feel he might have matured sufficently to take over in three years, but in the meantime needs to concentrate on ironing out his technical weaknesses as a wicketkeeper when standing up at the stumps.

The appointment of a captain is not something to be taken lightly. Decisions are easy to make, hard to undo. You are considering cricket's equivalent of a marriage between a man and a team, so the old saying 'marry in haste, repent at leisure' is particularly pertinent.

I am convinced cricket is entering an age where executive influence will be increasingly held by one individual – the manager. I have such a post at Yorkshire, Jackie Bond is in charge at Lancashire and Micky Stewart has done a marvellous job at Surrey. I would hope that we, and several others recently appointed, provide a glimpse into the future of the sport.

OPPOSITE *Alan Knott, a supreme wicketkeeper with a cricket brain that matched his agility*

At the moment the normal procedure for appointing a captain is for the cricket committee, known as the management committee in some counties, to make a recommendation to the

county club's full committee. This is usually ratified. A sensible enough system, but the people who make such a far-reaching decision must be in tune with the feelings of the county. That means watching a lot of cricket and talking to a lot of people.

Such commitment is sometimes impossible. This is why I think the manager is tailor-made to recommend a candidate to the cricket or management committee. He should know his players, their feelings and qualities. Committee men do a massive amount of unsung, unpaid work, but there is no substitute for day-to-day experience. I believe there are men in virtually every county who have a special insight into which players have the flair for captaincy.

Such a person was the late Arthur Mitchell, that well-respected Yorkshire coach. When I left my native county at the end of the 1968 season he stunned Doug Padgett by telling him: 'Take note. Illy will be captain of England in two years.'

No one else could have made such a statement, which of course came true. I confess I was amazed when I heard he had said it. At that time my experience as captain was limited to occasional matches in charge of Yorkshire. But Arthur had obviously spotted something in me which came to the attention of the selectors soon after I took over at Leicestershire.

OPPOSITE *A possible Yorkshire captain of the future, the ebullient David Bairstow, seen here running out Venkat on his Test debut*

3 Elementary...

It has become a national pastime to moan about the vagaries of the English climate. Summer? What summer? is the holiday-maker's lament. But the cricket captain has as much to complain about as those whose fortnight by the sea was turned into a soggy fiasco. A captain can be turned into a gibbering wreck by the unpredictability of our weather, which plays a vital role in any decision he has to make. It affects the pitch he has to judge and almost everything from the toss onwards.

The toss can be all important in English conditions, but it is sometimes a godsend to lose it. This is when your faith has to be placed in the helpful, but fallible, weather forecasters. I still shudder when I recall the 1972 series against Australia, when captaining England was made doubly difficult by the climate.

I won four tosses in that series, and would have gladly sold my soul to lose them. I was forced into a number of gambles I did not relish taking. In the First Test at Old Trafford, for instance, we were to play on a green grassy wicket with rain expected at 3 pm on the first day. Calculating that we would struggle before the rains came but have the advantage of bowling on a drying pitch after that, I batted first.

I was mortified when it stayed dry, but overcast. Whether it was divine retribution I did not know, but the rain lashed down within a three-mile radius of the ground. Those circumstances could easily have been fatal, but Australia did not exploit the helpful conditions and we won the match by 89 runs.

A wry grin for the camera as Phil Sharpe, John Edrich and myself shelter from the rain during the Second Test against New Zealand at Trent Bridge in 1973. Learning to live with the elements is an essential part of captaincy

That is just one indication of how luck can play a part in the toss. It is no exaggeration to say that any county captain will want to lose at least half of the tosses in a season. Of course, there are exceptions. It is always an advantage to win the toss when your inspection of the wicket reveals that it should break up and turn appreciably inside three days. Swansea, for example, was a traditional turner when I played for Yorkshire. Whereas Don Wilson, prone to nerves when he was expected to do well, literally had nightmares before we played there, I offered silent prayers that it would stay fine.

With the advent of the Surrey loam now used by many groundsmen as dressing for their wickets, there has been a reduction in the number of pitches that break up dramatically. However, a captain still wants to win the toss in a weekend match. The plan is usually to bat first on Saturday and hope the elements will work in your favour when the square is left exposed from Saturday evening until Monday morning.

Judging a pitch is one of the captain's most difficult tasks. Your thinking must be logical, but intuition and experience can sway your decision. Never forget any unusual incidents, such as the one I remember at The Oval, where Yorkshire batted first against Surrey on what everyone thought would be a benign wicket. Jim Laker was put on to enable the seamers to change around and to universal astonishment his third ball pitched outside the off-stump and went a good 18 inches down the leg-side for four byes. Tony Lock was immediately put on at the other end, and we were always fighting a losing battle after being bowled out cheaply.

In our post-match inquest we came to the conclusion that there was damp under the wicket which was sucked quickly to the surface. A simple solution, but devastatingly difficult to predict. It provided the perfect example of the hidden dangers of pitch reading. Despite my experience I would still only reckon to be correct in my analysis 90 per cent of the time.

Generally speaking, you can expect to play on four types of pitches in England. The pitch fast bowlers pray for has a hard surface covered by green strongly-rooted grass. This should have pace and bounce, and the ball will seam off the grass. No one likes to lose the toss in such circumstances, because you will be lucky to escape being put in. That usually condemns you to a first-innings struggle, especially if conditions are overcast.

A similarly firm surface, but covered by brown or straw-coloured grass, is also liable to aid the new-ball bowler. Yet because the grass does not contain the same moisture as our first example, it will not seam. The pitch might tend to break up insignificantly late in the match.

Spinners go through the whole spectrum of emotion from hope to despair when confronted by a square that is covered by a small amount of grass which has strong roots. It is deceptive.

Although it seems a foregone conclusion that this type of pitch will break up, the soil is often frustratingly bound together by the roots. Trent Bridge was a notorious example of this type, building up the hopes of slow bowlers and then giving them only a miserly amount of turn when it was too late to matter.

The final category, increasingly rare in this country, is stripped bare of grass with a surface akin to that of baked mud. The break-up of such a pitch, precipitated by the fast bowlers pounding the ball on to it, can be relied upon to start during the second day.

Countless pitches on the Indian subcontinent are, on the face of it, very like the last example. But getting batsmen out can be cricket's version of the Chinese water torture. This is because, although bare of grass, the wickets have a lot of roots. The bowlers consequently get no help at all.

A captain must take advantage of any clue nature sees fit to give him. Take care to study the amount and colour of the grass on the pitch, and the degree of moisture in it. This can be ascertained by the unscientific method of walking to the side of the square away from where the ball will pitch, and scratching away some of the surface with your studs. If the soil half an inch down is black there is some moisture to exploit. You can also be helped by the groundsman's daily ritual of rolling the square before play. Look closely. If the pitch gives under the weight of the roller, it will have some dampness in it.

Incidentally, a captain must tread warily about which roller he uses if he wins the toss on the first day of a three-day game. It is easy to make the mistake of asking for a heavy roller to be used, which can stimulate any moisture in the pitch and result in it coming to the surface faster than normal. This, of course, presents a needless opportunity to the opposing bowlers. If I have the slightest suspicion that there might be some deep-seated dampness in the pitch, I use a light roller before our innings.

A cricket ball will provide additional help in your rating of a pitch. If, when you bounce the ball on the pitch, it rises little more than a foot off the ground, it will be a slow, low wicket.

However, if it rebounds above waist height, the pace bowlers can start rubbing their hands in gleeful expectation of a profitable day's work. Experience, though, is the great tutor for any captain. You build up a mental file on the types of pitches you play on.

A captain has to stand or fall by his own judgement, and I prefer to look at the pitch individually and form my own opinions. If there is any doubt in my mind I send a senior player – Geoff Boycott helped me when we were England team-mates – out separately to reach his own conclusions. If we agree, the plan of action is simple. But if there is disagreement and doubts still linger, we go out to the middle together and explain why we came to contrasting decisions. In the end, though, there is only one man who can make the ultimate decision.

Local knowledge is important in assessing any pitch, whether at village or Test level. For instance I could not have failed to notice the distinct differences in conditions between Leicestershire, my former county, and Yorkshire. There is more rain in Yorkshire – if we are playing at Bradford the question is not whether it will rain, but how hard and from which direction – but Leicestershire weather has also posed its problems. It comes from the Birmingham area, and the county club had a meterological expert at Birmingham Airport always willing to give a short-range weather forecast. Bert Foord he might not have been, but he was accurate ... usually.

Whether he was a clandestine Kent supporter I do not know, but he certainly gifted them a five-wicket County Championship win at Grace Road in 1978. We were late starting on the first day, but the wicket was dry and the weather was improving. I felt the ball would move early on, and favoured putting Kent in. Our airport contact, however, oozed confidence when we rang him. 'It will be nice for the rest of the day', he predicted. 'But you will not bowl a ball tomorrow as there is a depression coming up.' One hasty change of mind later, I had won the toss and batted.

As I expected, batting was not easy, but we managed to struggle to 256-9 by the time our 100 overs ran out early on the

OPPOSITE *I will probably need that trusty umbrella now I am back at Yorkshire as team manager. Chris Old, Geoff Cope and captain John Hampshire seem resigned to the dampness*

second day. Surprised we were still playing? So were we. The expected downpour failed to materialize, and instead it was glorious, the best day of the summer. The airport man met our anguished queries of 'What the Hell happened?' by informing us that the wind had changed overnight, and the depression had gone south. The sun continued to beat down, the wicket got better and better, and Kent eventually scored 286 to win in 165 minutes. I spent the next week expecting to find out that our weather forecaster was Alan Ealham's brother-in-law!

Grace Road is rightly renowned as one of the best stages for batsmen in the country. Leicestershire play on excellent wickets, and it is almost a matter of course to bat after winning the toss. The ball swings less there than at almost any other venue on the county circuit. In Yorkshire the damper atmosphere is more receptive to swing, and the wickets are much greener. Headingley, for example, is one of the most disconcerting grounds to play on because of the unique effect cloud cover has there. The wicket can be full of runs, but the instant the sun is obscured the ball starts swinging.

We play at seaside resorts like Scarborough, where the ball has an alarming tendency to start swinging around teatime. The only explanation for that is the ebb and flow of the local tide, which must influence the amount of moisture in the air. Likewise the ball has been known to swing violently at Trent Bridge because of the proximity of the River Trent.

It is essential that the captain should understand as much as possible about the mysteries that surround the reasons why a ball swings. The scientists still try to convince cricketers that it is physically impossible for a ball to do so, but I prefer to believe my own eyes. The theory which has launched a whole generation of swing bowlers is that the ball will move in the air if shined on one side. The smooth half of the ball cuts through the atmosphere quicker and makes the ball swing. Atmospheric conditions have, obviously, to be heavy. But the baffling fact is that some balls simply swing more than others.

Cricketers, myself included, are sceptical of claims that, in this age of uniformity, every ball is essentially the same. I can always tell the difference between brands because as a spinner I have small hands and am able to tell the variations in size when I hold the ball between my fingers. For example the Kookaburra ball, which originated in Australia, has a slightly smaller seam than other makes and swings well early on. The Readers ball shines up well after the initial varnish has been knocked off, which means that it will start swinging again about ten overs into an innings. A captain has to know the particular properties of the ball he is expected to play with. Sometimes, if the ball is swinging late in the innings, it is better to delay taking the new ball.

There has been a growing chorus of media criticism of bowlers constantly asking the umpires to change a ball because it has gone out of shape. The cynical critic sees the bowler's plea as a ploy to try and get another ball in the hope that it will swing more. I totally reject that, and would place the blame on the manufacturers. In all my time in the game the standard has not been lower, and this can bring unfair advantages to the batting team. A bad ball goes soft, which negates the bowler's weapon of bounce. The stitching works itself loose,which means it is hard for a spinner to get between his fingers. The only time this poor quality works in favour of the fielding side is when their opponents are chasing runs on an easy-paced wicket and the soft ball does not come on to the bat.

The elements can influence the balance of a side, especially when the selection of the bowlers for a three-day game is considered. I tend to favour the more conservative policy of always having two spinners in the side, as they can be match winners when the weather is unsettled. 'Deadly' Derek Underwood, for instance, has become synonymous with the ability of the slower bowler to capitalize on a drying wicket.

One-day cricket, that child of the modern era, conceived to cater for the public's growing demand for instant results, is a completely different ball-game. It has thrown up a new type of tactical decision that has to be made. I enjoyed quite some

success with Leicestershire in the sphere of limited-overs competition and was fortunate in having a good team able to adapt to ever-changing demands.

The current fashion among county captains if they win the toss in a one-day game is to insert opponents. This is a sound and sensible ploy when the wicket is likely to give initial help to the bowlers. In such circumstances it is very difficult for the side with first knock to set themselves a realistic target. The common failing is for them to be too ambitious, and pay for that by throwing away wickets on a needless run chase. The side batting second has the undoubted advantage of knowing exactly what is required of them.

However, I am convinced it is worth taking the calculated risk of batting first if the wicket is good and there is adequate light. Sensible batting in those conditions can be rewarded by a sizeable total which acts as a pyschological barrier to your opponents. The captain must order his specialist batsmen to eliminate silly risks, and concentrate on building a base which can be built on in the last 15 overs. That period is the time for acceleration, and with controlled, aggressive batting often realizes more than 100 runs.

I would have adopted that policy in the 1979 Gillette Cup final, when Northamptonshire captain Jim Watts made the fatal mistake of asking Somerset to bat first in perfect conditions. Predictably inspired by Viv Richards, Somerset made 269-8, which was always enough. It is easy to be wise after the event, but if I were Watts I would have had more faith in the ability of my batsmen to set Somerset a formidable total. The whole cricket world knew Brian Rose's team were under pressure, going for their first major honour. I believe they would have cracked when faced with chasing a daunting total.

That Gillette wicket at Lord's was obviously going to be a corker. But there are occasions when you do not know how many runs will be enough to give you a chance of victory until you bat. This is where an experienced opening batsman can help his captain.

OPPOSITE *'Deadly' Derek Underwood. A study of style, concentration and determination*

This picture could so easily have shown Northants captain Jim Watts holding the Gillette Cup, but his tactical mistakes allowed man-of-the-match Viv Richards and Somerset skipper Brian Rose to share the limelight

Micky Norman, the former Leicestershire right-hander, quickly impressed me as a good judge of how many runs a one-day wicket would be likely to yield. Knowing there is no substitute for experience out in the middle, I made a point of asking for his opinion as soon as he was dismissed. After our discussions I would then instruct the later batsmen how to pace the innings.

A captain must remember that he is involved in a constantly changing situation. A 2 pm assessment of the wicket is no guarantee you will know how it is playing 90 minutes later. I remember Northamptonshire thinking they had a great chance of winning at Grace Road for the first time when they got us out for 182 in a Gillette Cup game. I was virtually an oasis of confidence in a dressing-room desert of pessimism. During my innings I had noticed the ball was not coming on to the bat with the ease it had earlier, and felt our four seam bowlers could win the match for us. Thankfully, I was proved right. Northamptonshire, to their eternal disgust, were skittled for 62 by some fine bowling spearheaded by Ken Higgs and Norman McVicker.

A captain must be aware of the ways bowlers are helped by the direction in which the wind is blowing. A breeze from fine leg, which helps an off-spinner float the ball away from the batsman, also aids the outswing bowler. Logically, the inswing specialist is helped by a wind from third man.

A child can calculate the wind direction. All you need to do is to go out to the square and study which way a handkerchief flutters. The only precaution necessary is not to make the test near a pavilion, where the winds tends to swirl. So, the next time you see a man waving a white hankie he is not surrendering, only planning the battle.

4 Look and Learn

Every batsman is involved in a grail-like search for perfection. None find it, so a captain must be looking to learn about the fallibilities of each individual. When a failing in temperament or technique is spotted, it is essential it is committed to memory. There is nothing better for bowlers to be captained by a man who has trained his mind to be a cricket computer that can instantly summon up information about a particular player.

Obviously it takes time to build up a mental file on opponents. But if you have any designs on leadership, remember you are never too young to learn. For instance, you do not have to be a gnarled veteran to assess the implication of the batsman's grip. As I mentioned earlier, the way a batsman holds the bat gives a clue about his favourite shots. Those whose right hand is underneath the back of the handle are far more likely to be square cutters and on-side players than those who favour the orthodox grip, which encourages freer shots through the covers.

Glenn Turner, for example, used to expose his initial vulnerability because of the unusual way he held the bat, with the top hand behind the handle. This grip needlessly restricted his natural talent, making him primarily an off-side player who could be tied down by accurate bowling at his leg and middle stumps.

Glenn, as conscientious as he is classy, gradually became aware of this while playing for Worcestershire on the county circuit, and during one winter in New Zealand remodelled his grip. I adopted my traditional tactics in our next meeting, a Benson and Hedges Cup match, only to be surprised when Glenn

began flipping me over mid-wicket with effortless ease. He had proved his dedication by recognizing a fault and working on becoming a shot-maker on both sides of the wicket. It was back to the drawing board for me.

I was fortunate that I had a wealth of experience in county cricket when I took up my first full-time post as captain of Leicestershire in 1969. Having first-hand knowledge of players' strengths and weaknesses was an inestimable aid to field setting, and enabled me to advise young bowlers like Paddy Clift, John Steel and Peter Booth.

One of my first acts when captaining any side is to remind my bowlers that they have an equal duty to remember anything they learn about a batsman. Too many players, at all levels, allow invaluable information to go in one ear and out the other. They must realize that they cannot expect to be wet-nursed by the skipper.

I occasionally despaired of Richard Hutton, the former Yorkshire and England all-rounder who now lives in Johannesburg. He seemed surprised at the value of remembering any snippet of knowledge. That was summed up after one match at Eastbourne, when we combined to capitalize on the weaknesses of the developing Tony Greig.

In his early days with Sussex Greig had a damaging love of hitting the ball on the up early in his innings. I advised Richard to bowl just short of a length three or four inches outside the off-stump, calculating that Greig would edge an intended drive to slip. The instructions were followed perfectly, and within two overs Greig, showing suicidal lack of restraint, had nicked one to slip. In the same match we had him caught slashing at a bouncer.

In the dressing room later Richard could not contain his enthusiasm. 'If I had you fielding at mid-off to me I would get an extra 50 wickets a season', he told me. I encourage my players to be enthusiastic, but seized the opportunity to lecture Richard on the need to remember what he had learned. Otherwise, I told him, a captain might just as well talk to himself.

OPPOSITE *Glenn Turner, a batsman whose talent is equalled by his dedication*

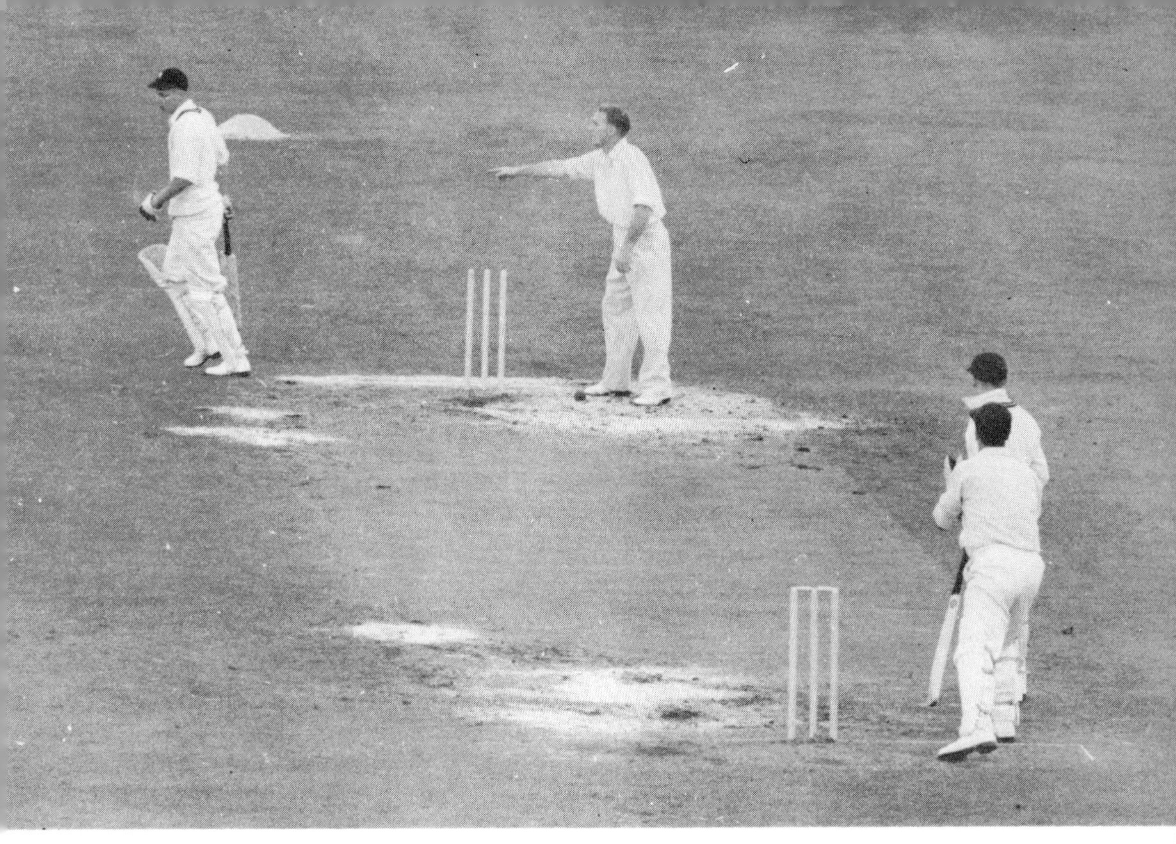

Johnny Wardle was often a controversial figure in my early days at Yorkshire, but I respected his knowledge. Just one pearl of advice from him made me a far better bowler.

Like countless raw bowlers in the process of learning their trade, I used to bowl one bad ball an over, which invariably went for four. Wardle took it upon himself to impress on me that only total concentration would eliminate such a flaw from my game. The turning point came when we played Warwickshire at Edgbaston, and Wardle fielded mid-off to me throughout a 12-over spell. His advice came after every ball and consisted of a single, forcibly-expressed word: 'CONCENTRATE'. I did just that, and to my delight went through the spell without a wayward delivery. 'There,' he said. 'I have proved my point. Never forget this lesson.' I didn't.

ABOVE *Johnny Wardle, a temperamental character whose knowledge of the game demanded respect. He is seen here after kicking the ball on to the stumps to run out South African opener Trevor Goddard.*

OPPOSITE *Richard Hutton, an occasionally exasperating bowler to captain*

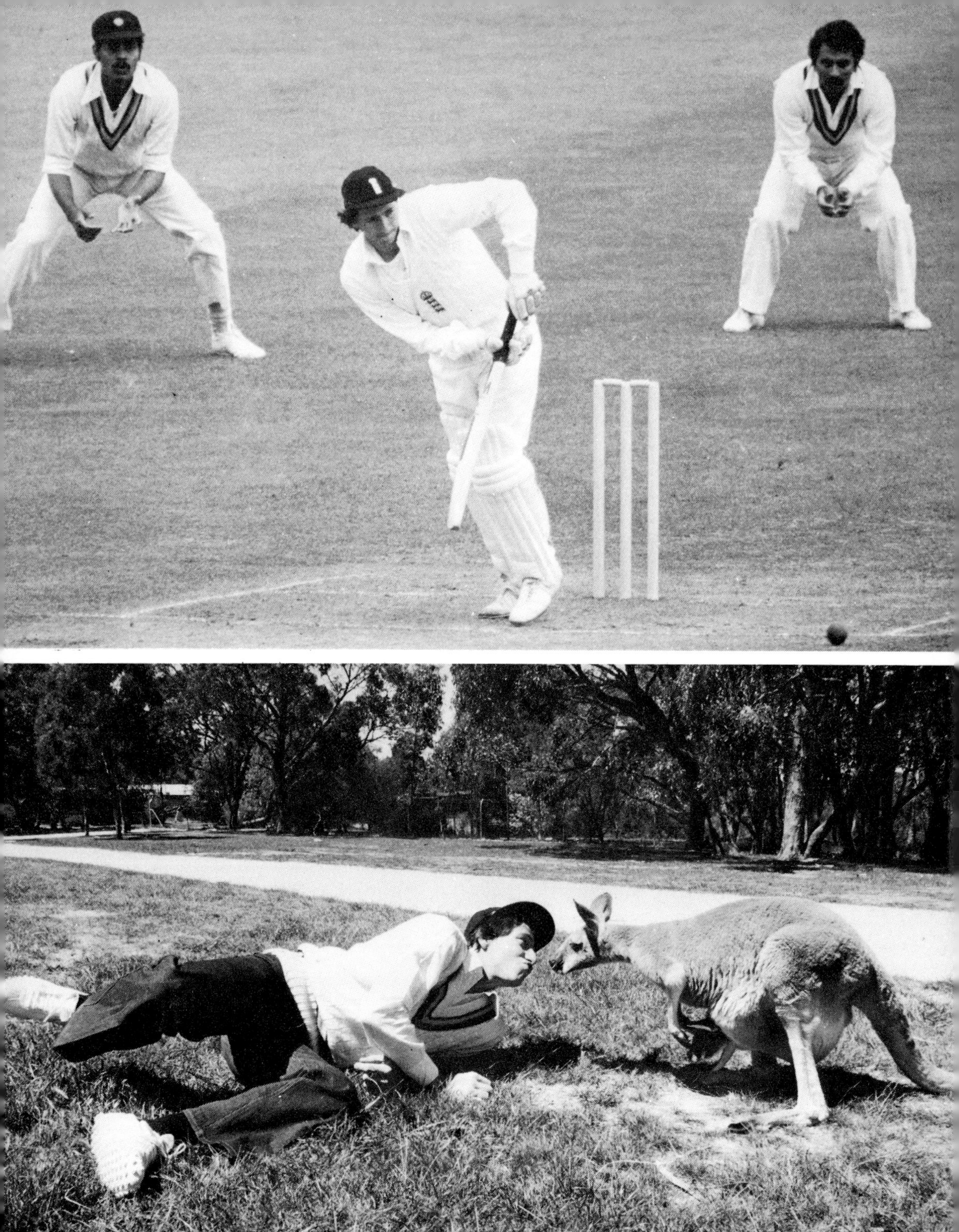

Getting a batsman out boils down to exploiting either a physical or pyschological failing. On the technical side, therefore, the captain has to recognize the limitations of his opponent, and decide whether to attack any strengths he has. An accomplished on-side player can be countered by bowling wide of the off-stump, but it is sometimes worth feeding the favourite shots and rearranging your field in the hope of a catch.

The mysterious workings of the human mind always give you a chance. You will come across many different temperaments and everything from nervousness to over-confidence can lead to a batsman's downfall.

Derek Randall typifies the batsman who lives on his nerves at the start of an innings. His tension comes out in his inability to stand still and the apparent nonsense he says to himself while at the crease. He rarely made runs against Leicestershire when I was captain because we piled on the pressure by crowding four men around the bat. Randall could almost smell their aftershave and, feeling hopelessly restricted, went for foolish shots, especially the hook, which he has yet to master.

Ian Botham, in contrast, brims with confidence. Somerset's young Samson of English cricket is seemingly destined to rewrite the record books, but in his early days could be made to pay for the rashness of youth. Patience was not a virtue Ian possessed when he came into county cricket, and instead of quietly playing himself in he would be looking to open those massive shoulders and hit you out of the ground. Being caught in the deep taught him that conservatism is not a sin, and he became a better player for it.

Barry Richards also felt it was virtually his duty to score off every ball. It was one of the few chinks in his formidable armour. An off-spinner turning the ball into him from just outside the off-stump would always have a chance because he would usually accept the challenge and try to hit through square cover.

Richards was not the type of batsman who could graft doggedly away to a century on a turning pitch like Geoff Boycott. However, 'Thatch', as he has been nicknamed by England

OPPOSITE *The two faces of Derek Randall. The nervous, fidgety character at the crease (above) is totally different from the relaxed individual off the field (below)*

colleague Botham following his hair transplant, can fall prey to his occasionally excessive caution.

A bowler could put his mortgage on Boycott not attempting to hit him over the top early in his stay at the crease. The way to frustrate Geoff into submission is to deploy the field to stop the singles that are his main way of scoring before fully settled in. As a spinner I would attack Geoff by having men very close to the bat on both sides in front of the wicket. They would be ready to snap up bat-and-pad chances, which he is prone to offer.

Viv Richards, whose class, like Boycott's, has been proved in Test cricket, is not perfect. He is vulnerable to the ball leaving him in the off-stump area. Fred Trueman, bowling off his three-quarter run, would have caused him a lot of problems with his ability to move the ball through the air.

However, all the theory in the world is useless if you cannot make it work when it matters. I remember playing Somerset at Taunton in 1978, when some hasty planning was necessary when Richards appeared well set at lunch. I collared Les Taylor, the promising Leicestershire pace bowler, and told him to make his fourth ball after the interval a big bouncer outside Richard's off-stump. I then instructed Paddy Clift, who was fielding at long leg to move ten yards wider and on to the boundary edge for that particular delivery. I reasoned that Viv would not be able to resist the temptation of hooking, and would hit the ball down Paddy's throat. My preparations were so painstaking I took the trouble to tell both bowler and fielder that if there was a no-ball the plan would still be put into operation on the fourth delivery.

Sure enough, Les bowled a no-ball with his second delivery. But when the fourth came it was perfect. Viv rose to the bait and hooked it straight towards where Paddy should have been. Instead, our quiet Rhodesian was ten yards away. It would be an understatement to say I was peeved, especially as Richards went on to make 99. What really ruined my blood pressure was Paddy's whispered apology that he had miscounted. What is it they say about the best-laid plans of mice and men?...

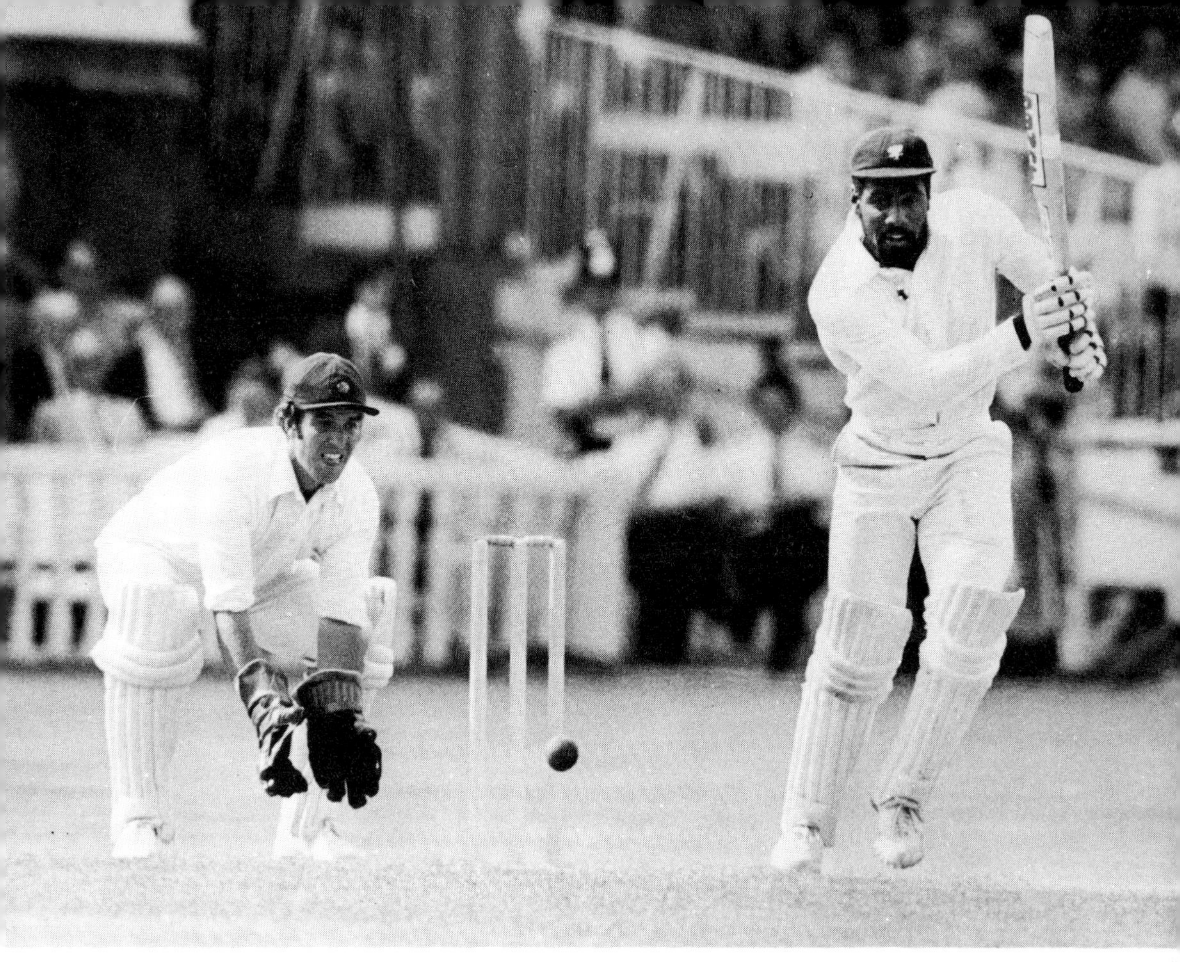

Viv Richards on his way to the century which helped Somerset win their first major honour – the 1979 Gillette Cup. A superb batsman, but he has his weaknesses in the off-stump area

Schemes like that are the lifeblood of a captain and his bowlers. Without hope, they may as well all jump out of the highest pavilion window. At times when things have not been going quite right I have consoled myself with the thought that at least all the great batsmen have their weak points.

The most illustrious Achilles heel I exposed as a captain was that of Sir Gary Sobers, the greatest player in my era. He had the natural flamboyance of a West Indian, but allied that to the type of bulldog grit and determination which has seen countless Englishmen through a crisis. Unlike most of his compatriots, he could retain a dignified assurance when batting on a turning wicket. Yet in 1969, after my first series as England captain, Sobers was being written off as a fading force. That all stemmed from my hunch that he would be prepared to flirt with danger – in his case a half-volley well outside the off-stump. Barry Knight of Leicestershire could produce that particular delivery to order, Gary could not resist a dart at it, and was often caught in the slips by Phil Sharpe. The effectiveness of the ploy was such that Gary overcompensated for his failing, going too far across in order to rule out the possibility of an edge and consequently dragging the ball on.

It is no idle exaggeration to say that a shrewd piece of planning can change the course of cricket history. But for two dropped catches the influential career of Ian Chappell could have been nipped in the bud. 'Chappelli' had a miserable start to the Ashes series of 1970-71. We were more than happy to feed his penchant for the hook, and devised a scheme to take full advantage of the slashing shot he also favoured. This involved having Basil d'Oliveira at third man, almost behind third slip some fifteen yards in from the boundary. He was placed so perfectly that several times he did not have to move when the Australians recklessly slashed at the short ball.

Having been caught out slashing and hooking, Chappell – and several of his team-mates – had plenty to think about. Faced with John Snow bowling chest high from just short of a length, Chappell began to get too square-on, with the result that the ball would take the outside edge and go towards third slip. In the Fifth Test at Melbourne Snowy bowled magnificently to find the edge – but was let down by some uncharacteristic fielding by Colin Cowdrey. He dropped Chappell on 0 and 14, two of five slip chances he squandered in the match. Chappell capitalized on the let off to score 111 and rescue his reputation. I am positive another failure at Melbourne would have led to him being dropped for the rest of a series that ended with him as Australian captain.

OPPOSITE *Colin Cowdrey's complex character made him ultimately unsuited to captaincy*

Cowdrey himself was an unwilling guinea-pig for the theory

that strategy can destroy a great batsman. Brian Close and myself recognized that, although he was a superb player, Cowdrey was not a good starter. He preferred to spend some time quietly judging the pace of the pitch, defending by the negative technique of pushing forward with bat and pad locked firmly together. This policy invariably produces the occasional ricochet, but Cowdrey, an acknowledged master of bat-pad, got away with it because his reputation ensured he was never crowded. This illogical reverence was ended when Closey and I devised our counter to him. It involved me bowling, and having Closey squatting suicidally close to the bat at silly mid-off. Unused to having a fielder breathing down his neck, Cowdrey would lose his characteristic composure. He would complain to the umpire that Brian was moving, and hardly relished the reply from the balding figure on his haunches: 'If you played properly with your bloody bat instead of your pad I would not have to stand here.'

In the end Cowdrey found it imposssible to defend against me with Brian waiting vulture-like for any mistake. He resorted to charging down the wicket – a fatal mistake, as it was not his style – and was stumped several times. He was the most spectacular victim of that ploy, although Ken Barrington was similarly unsettled and tried to escape being bogged down by hitting injudiciously across the line.

Cowdrey's problem with the silly mid-off policy was ninety per cent mental. He was lucky it only cost him his wicket. Psychological problems could have cost Dennis Amiss his life. I am convinced that, if protective helmets had not been introduced, Amiss would now be dead. A strong statement, I know, but one which illustrates the depth of my concern for a man I regard as a friend.

Some four years ago Dennis was a demoralized batsman. Acutely aware of his problems against fast bowling, he had completely lost his nerve. It startled me to see him being bounced into submission by bowlers who had no pretentions above medium pace. Yet whenever Amiss saw the ball was short he ducked and turned his head away, never looking at its flight. Inevitably, he was hit. Many other times the ball whistled within a fraction of an inch of his cowering frame. I am certain that if he had gone out to play World Series Cricket in that state of mind he would not have come back alive. For someone unnerved by bowlers like Ken Higgs regularly to face Packer's battery of fast bowlers would have been as suicidal as putting a gun to his own head.

It saddened me, but as a captain I had to exploit that transparent weakness in a batsman who had proved himself a big-innings player at the top level. The harsh creed of professional sport is that dog must eat dog, and my bowlers could not wait to get at him. Coming from Yorkshire, one of the hardest schools of cricket, I understood their reasons.

But I could not stop myself offering some heartfelt advice when we played Warwickshire at Coventry. I was blunt and to the point when the bobbing and weaving began. 'For Christ's sake Dennis, look at the ball', I implored. I did not want him to get seriously hurt. Thankfully the wearing of helmets came just in time. Amiss's confidence has been restored, but he must realize how close he came to becoming one of the most tragic figures in the history of first-class cricket.

One of the most amusing, yet at the same time frustrating, products of the mental pressure in cricket are the 'rabbits' every bowler has. The effect on some batsmen can be so drastic they are considering their dressing-room excuse the moment their tormentor comes on to bowl.

In my early days I developed the happy knack of dismissing Ted Dexter cheaply. He had a habit of playing half forward, leaving me a gate to bowl through. I used regularly to get rid of Basil d'Oliveira in similar fashion. He was essentially a back-foot player and my slightly quicker delivery could squeeze between bat and pad. Basil, though, knows the thrill of being the hunter as well as the misery of being the hunted. In the 1970 Rest of the World series he quickly made Graeme Pollock his prized rabbit, beating him with the ball that came back into him.

A sadly familiar sequence concerning Dennis Amiss, whose crisis of confidence against pace bowling could have proved more serious but for the advent of helmets. In the photograph on the right he recoils after being hit by a Sarfraz bouncer during The Oval Test of 1974; the centre photograph shows Pakistan captain Intikhab stemming the flow of blood with his handkerchief; in the photograph on the far right Amiss, the cut on his cheek caused by the seam of the ball clearly visible, is led off for further treatment. A captain has to exploit transparent weaknesses, no matter what he feels emotionally in the matter

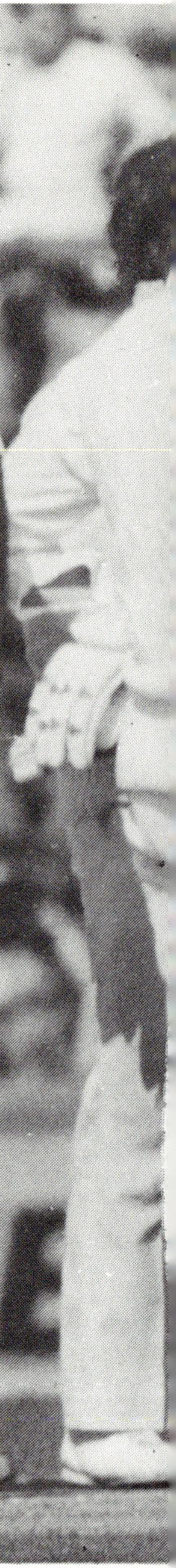

Overseas players, especially South Africans, seem vulnerable to that type of delivery. Men like Mike Procter, Barry Richards and Clive Rice tend to hit the ball going away from them with more power and assurance. This goes against the traditional thinking that a batsman is in greater danger from the ball leaving him. Looked at logically, he cannot use his pads as a second line of defence, which enables a captain confidently to post slips to snap up the edges.

One of the eternal puzzles of my long career in first-class cricket was the hold Sonny Ramadhin had on me. He got me out in ways I did not credit as possible. For instance he dismissed me in successive Test matches when I padded up at harmless deliveries going down the leg-side. To my horror the ball hit the top of my pad and was deflected on to the off-stump. I have never been out like that again.

However, you can fight against the sheer illogicality of the whole business. I remember turning Barry Dudleston's dread of facing Sarfraz, Northamptonshire's Pakistan paceman, to Leicestershire's advantage. We needed a good start to our victory chase in the last innings, and 'Danny' frankly admitted he doubted his potential to overcome the hoodoo. As the wicket was taking turn we agreed it would be better to send David Gower, then a little uncertain against spin, to see off Sarfraz. That was achieved in Gower's bright and breezy style. Danny's defensive technique on an increasingly difficult pitch proved vital when he came in after Gower's dismissal, and we won in a canter.

After that another note was added to the Illingworth mental file....

5 In the Field

There has to be a bit of Montgomery or Napoleon in any successful cricket captain. The qualities needed to do well, whether on the field of battle or field of play, are exactly the same. Each job calls for astute handling of men, and the best possible deployment of forces available.

Remember that matches are often won or lost by a side's performance in the field. The team must be well organized and able to adapt instantly to given circumstances. A captain's task, superficially, is to know the positions in which to place his fielders. This can be learned in a coaching manual. What is more important is to realize the individual temperaments of the bowlers you work with. You must tie their ideas and attitudes in with your own.

When I led Leicestershire I had tactical disagreements with off-spinner Jackie Birkenshaw. He does not like having too many men around the bat when he starts bowling, preferring to settle down and find his length and line. He is at his happiest bowling tightly, frustrating the batsman until he holes out in the deep. In contrast I was eager to have close fielders both as a captain and bowler. Jackie and I reached the traditional British compromise over our differences, as he was allowed one or two overs to attune himself to the conditions before I tightened the screw by bringing the fielders in.

I cannot stress enough the importance of recognizing individual traits like those of Jackie, which I consider to stem from a basic lack of confidence. Some bowlers, inhibited by having men around the bat, become too conscious of them and bowl badly.

One of the secrets of good captaincy is knowing when, and how much, to attack or defend. I believe it is imperative to attack all new batsmen, especially if they are established players. If a recognized batsman offers an early chance, it is vital to have the close fielders capable of accepting it. Otherwise your opponent might gain confidence from his let-off, and ease into an ominously fluent rhythm.

It goes without saying that a captain is in the hands of his bowlers. Should he seize the initiative by posting men in attacking positions the gesture is worthless if the bowler perfoms badly. Nevertheless, I would advise any captain to be positive early on. Do not panic if the occasional ball is dispatched to the ropes. Sensible perseverance is a virtue.

A captain with attacking intentions would probably post at least two slips and a gully to aid the seamers early on. If you have a confident top-class fast bowler you might be able to bowl with only one man on the off-side, stationed at cover point. Chris Old of Yorkshire is one who feels secure enough to bowl without a mid-off, who in that situation strengthens the slip cordon.

I applaud initiative, but a captain must be wary of such a field setting. My reluctance is based on seeing many medium pacers becoming too aware of that gap in the off-side field. Knowing they can be driven expensively through mid-off, they tend to be afraid of pitching the ball up. Bowling a yard short does not give the ball a chance to swing, and is a warning sign that must be heeded. I feel it is probably better to keep your mid-off, especially at club level, and make do with the two slips, gully and a wicketkeeper, which is where 80 per cent of the catching chances go anyway.

At the highest level there are the variations in conditions in the various countries to consider. A Test in England usually features three or four slips for the first eight or ten overs, but then men are gradually dispatched to mid-wicket and mid-off. This leaves your team in a semi-attacking position, but able to save the singles.

However, in Australia the gap between attack and defence is more sharply defined. There is a greater commitment to attack with the new ball or when a new batsman comes to the crease. But when a batsman appears well set, defence is the overriding object. English conditions, with greener wickets and more movement, are more conducive to some degree of positive cricket.

The current trend in all spheres of the game has placed the accent on the negative ability of being able to contain your opponents. This obsessive attitude towards run-saving is a by-product of the demands of limited-overs cricket. Unfortunately it is is having far-reaching consequences.

Even in the local Leagues, where clubs are becoming increasingly aware of the importance of results, the captains worship the modern god of containment. They have been conditioned by watching televized one-day cricket, and follow the first-class attitudes like sheep. I cannot hide my sadness at that, because I still value the principles that were drummed into me as a lad. I felt it was a sin not to try and take a wicket with every ball I bowled. This is just not happening any more.

We have gone badly astray. Certainly the three major limited-overs competitions – John Player League, Gillette Cup and Benson and Hedges Cup – bring in cash that is cricket's lifeline. But the cost cannot be registered in any balance sheet. Even the County Championship, with the artificial 100-overs limit in each first innings, is being contaminated by the attitudes conceived in the one-day game. Far too many captains, seeing their side bowl 80 overs at a cost of, say, 200 runs, are content to sacrifice bowling bonus points. For the last 20 overs they adopt Sunday League style field placing.

I believe the arbitrary 100-overs limit should be abolished, in an attempt to encourage more attacking cricket. Faced with a situation where the side batting first can extend its innings for as long as it likes, the fielding captain would have little alternative but to order his bowlers to attack. Bowling sides out would again be the main objective.

The biggest culprit for the current spate of defensive cricket

One of the perks of the job. Leicestershire secretary Mike Turner sprays me with champagne as we begin celebrating our John Player League title win of 1974

is the John Player League. At least in the other two longer one-day competitions there is a need to attempt to snatch early wickets. But common sense dictates to a captain that he cannot expect to bowl a side out in 40 overs on a reasonably good wicket. This has led to a new breed of bowlers ignoring the worth of taking wickets. Tim Lamb, of Northamptonshire, is one of several relatively inexperienced bowlers who have gone on record as saying they concentrate solely on keeping the runs down.

My criticism may seem strange considering I led Leicestershire to the John Player title in 1974 and 1977. Of course, I was as aware as anyone of the need to save runs on Sunday. But it was always my policy to bowl at the stumps. I concede this consisted of aiming at the leg peg, but at least if the batsman had missed the ball it would have hit the wicket.

I am also proud I brought a modicum of attack into my field setting, being one of the few captains who believed in the value of posting slips on Sunday if the ball was moving. I took the virtually unprecedented step of having two slips throughout the spells of Les Taylor and Ken Higgs in one John Player match at Swansea.

The normal, less adventurous, policy is to have at least three men on the boundary at the start of a 40-over innings, and no-one apart from the wicketkeeper in close catching positions. This has hidden, but very real, dangers for our budding batsmen. On Sunday a shot through the slip area is a valuable run-producing weapon. In the Championship it is disastrous, and many young batsmen find it hard to break out of their limited-overs habit.

I am not one to be lulled into a false sense of security, and I recognize that there are also many things wrong in the three-day game. I have been concerned about the declining standards of captaincy when it comes to declarations. Some skippers seem to be living in cloud cuckoo land when they set their targets. I never cease to be amazed when a captain of a side that struggled to average two runs an over suddenly asks his opponents to make in the region of eight runs an over to win. Caution? That is hardly the word. If he applied the principles of his declaration to the rest of the life he would refuse to get out of bed for fear of being run over by a double-decker bus.

I can confidently say that in my time at Leicestershire we had a result in at least 50 per cent of the matches where I made a declaration. My equation of fairness is that you should not ask a side to score more than four runs an over if in the rest of the game the teams have averaged around two. That is double the mean scoring rate and gives both sides a realistic chance.

Even then that is no guarantee a team will make a reasonable bid for victory. The fear that grips some individuals prevented a number of captains chasing four an over at Grace Road, where the perfect state of the wicket was reflected in previous scoring rates in excess of three an over during the rest of the game.

The counter argument that teams have improved their run-chasing ability because of the demands of the limited-overs game is a fair one. In addition I realize the introduction of the statutory 20 overs in the last hour has made it easier for the chasing team, who can pace their reply. Any county side entering the final hour with wickets in hand and only 100 or so to make will be quietly confident.

Indeed, I would have backed almost any first-class team to succeed where the Indians narrowly failed in the final Test at The Oval in summer 1979. India were not used to such a situation, made basic errors – Vishwanath should have come in at his normal position to take the pressure off double-century-maker Gavaskar – and ended nine runs short of an historic win. A county side would have won with four overs to spare.

That is just one example of the specialized skills the one-day game has promoted. Captains have also had to become more flexible in their field setting and able to make instant decisions. In first-class cricket it is increasingly common for a captain to be faced with the dilemma of what to do when the opponents need a run a ball to win. This requirement tends to be taken literally, with the batsmen running at any opportunity. If twelve runs are needed off the last two overs it is advisable to have at least six close fielders able to stop the quick single. If that proves successful, and no runs come from the next three deliveries, two of the six fielders can drop a little deeper. But both captain and his team must be able to react to fluctuation in fortunes. A boundary usually means the field has to be brought in again.

These tight, tense finishes provide a tough test of everyone's nerves. Stress must be lived with because understandable human failings can prove dear. One player freezing under the most intense pressure ultimately cost Leicestershire the 1978 John Player League title.

Somerset wanted one to win off the final ball of our Sunday match at Glastonbury and no-one needed reminding of the importance of keeping cool. I ushered my players in and stated the obvious – that the batsmen would run whatever the circumstances. The consultations over, I went to short leg, took a deep breath, and we were away. Les Taylor, the bowler, followed my instruction to the letter, pitching the ball well up to batsman Phil Slocombe. He hit the ball fifteen yards to Brian Davison at cover, and the ball was in the fielder's hand before the batsmen began to scramble. Then, to my horror, things began to go wrong. 'Davo', obviously realizing his best chance was to throw to the bowler's end, hesitated when he saw no one was backing up there. Instead of a simple job, he had to throw at the stumps, and missed by inches. As the ball went past the wicket Slocombe was still two yards out, but we lost whatever chance remained when Peter Booth remained frozen four yards away at mid-on.

It was the classic example of an inexperienced player being overwhelmed by the occasion. Throughout the whole affair he did not move, and had to be criticized afterwards. Harsh maybe, but Booth's action, or lack of it, cost us a tie that would have given us two points more than Hampshire, the eventual champions, and four more than runners-up Somerset, who finished one place above us.

Peter, hopefully, will remember the painful lesson he learned that day. Limited-overs cricket has taught me several things, not least never to give up hope.

You could not have got a price on Leicestershire when Kent, with plenty of wickets in hand, needed only fifteen runs in six overs to win a John Player clash at Grace Road in 1977. Bernard Julien was 81 not out, and clearly relishing finding form on a perfect batting pitch.

I knew Bernard would love to end the game in spectacular style, and told Jackie Birkenshaw to toss the ball up to him. I realized a safety-first approach was useless, and did not hold out a great deal of hope of success for that particular ploy. It was very much the last throw of a desperate gambler. Jackie's first delivery was lashed for six, but I told him to persevere. Three balls later Julien fell into our trap, caught in the deep attempting to emulate his earlier blow.

The door, apparently shut tight before, was ajar. It opened further when Jackie sowed the seeds of panic by taking two more quick wickets. Kent lost all their composure and with the aid of a last-gasp run-out we triumphed by two runs. It all stemmed from our faint hopes that Julien would not be able to control his natural flamboyance.

There is no doubt that one-day competition is behind the dramatic improvement in the fielding standards of English cricket. But there is a danger of club captains being influenced too much by this, and overestimating the ability of their fielders. They are indeed fortunate if they have men with three-quarters of the gazelle-like speed and grace of Derek Randall and David Gower.

I would advise any captain in club cricket to recognize the limitations of his players by setting a staggered field. That involves having mid-wicket and cover five yards nearer the bat than in county cricket, and some men being stationed further out. It increases the likelihood of preventing the sprinted single, and adds to the pressure on the batsmen. They would have to calculate how to hit the ball over the close field without reaching those men a little deeper.

At whatever level you play it is crucial to have your team well drilled in the field. A good captain should train his players into glancing at him three times an over. This gives him the perfect opportunity to make slight field changes.

When these changes become necessary they should be as discreetly directed as possible. Nothing is worse than seeing a captain gesticulating wildly or bawling like some terrace lout. One of my first points to any side is to outline my insistence on a responsible, professional attitude in the field. That stems from the chastening experience of a 28-over Sunday game at Nottingham early in my Leicestershire career.

It was a typical finish with runs at a premium and the side dotted around the boundary. Problems arose when I wanted to summon a fielder in from deep cover to stop the possibility of the batsman taking more than one run from a shot in that direction. I was 150 yards away at deep mid-wicket and, to the delight of the crowd, had to yell myself hoarse. I read the riot act afterwards. My message was simple – all that was needed was for them to look at me occasionally and take notice of simple signals. That is the sort of organization that enhances the reputation of any team.

A captain should adopt a sensible, mature attitude when tackling the important task of bringing on the young bowlers under his wing. He must be like a gardener, always giving that extra bit of attention to the plant that is struggling to establish itself. Each variety of bowler needs specialist care.

I am worried at the number of captains from all walks of cricket life who overbowl promising young fast bowlers. Spells of 20 overs in an afternoon have been known in club cricket, and I recoiled in dismay last summer when I read Kent had allowed Graham Dilley, their pace prospect, to bowl 30 overs in an innings. There is always the possibility that a young fast bowler, although fit and strong, will lose that vital extra yard of pace if overbowled. Both clubs and counties must realize that a potential strike bowler should not be made to do the donkey work.

Eager, talented strike bowlers are the rare stones in the bowling crown. They must be nurtured carefully. John Snow, for instance, rebelled and lost his enthusiasm because he was bowled too much. I recognized this, and told him he would be used only in short bursts. Similarly, when Bob Willis, then a gangling youngster, flew out to replace Alan Ward in the England squad for the 1970-71 Ashes tour, he was never on for more than five overs at a time. He would not have lasted the tour had he been forced into lengthier spells.

The medium pacers are the workhorses of any team, and by saying that I do not wish to decry their influence. But the very essence of being a valuable medium pacer is the ability to bowl long, unselfish stints without complaint. A captain must give the young medium pacer the chance to prove his stamina.

The spinner is a more sensitive cricketer who needs the utmost consideration. I have pledged that if Yorkshire discover a talented young spinner I will not play him in one-day cricket for at least

three years. A slow bowler requires time to develop his craft, to learn about variations in flight and pace, and the value of length and line. This can only happen by bowling long spells in three-day matches. That is difficult enough, without being exposed to the potentially confusing demands of the one-day game, which call for the more experienced spinner, well aware of the need to push the ball through slightly quicker than normal.

Obviously the captain knows more about field placing than the emerging bowler. He should never dictate, yet make sure he gets his own way. A skipper needs to be tactful, first asking the bowler for his thoughts and then supplementing those ideas with the knowledge of his own experience. In that way a bowler is learning to think for himself, an essential part of a cricket education.

There will always be times of frustration when you are in the field. But the captain should ceaselessly contemplate ways to break through. Never be afraid to try the unexpected. I did that in my third match as England captain, the Headingley Test of 1969, which is when I consider most of my qualities as a leader came together.

The West Indies needed 303 to win, had plenty of time and the use of a pitch that was getting better as time went on. They cruised past 200 for the loss of three wickets, and I felt I had to make a move when Clive Lloyd came to the crease.

It would have been logical to let Derek Underwood continue to bowl at Lloyd, as his confidence had been boosted by the earlier wickets of Camacho and Butcher. He was not happy when I took over from him, but I reckoned Underwood was more vulnerable to a typical Lloyd blitz, which could have tilted the balance irrevocably. I quickly had Lloyd caught behind, and wasted no time in bringing back Derek to wrap up victory.

The greatest advice any captain can be given is never to be frightened of losing your job, whether that be the leadership of Chorlton-cum-Hardy thirds or England. I certainly never had any fears about being sacked from the national team.

If I had been afraid of losing my position as England captain

OPPOSITE *Bob Willis – a fine fast bowler who needed gentle handling*

I would have made nervous mistakes and not lasted a year. As it was, I had the confidence to make my own decisions, was never wary of the consequences of attack, and lasted for 36 Tests between 1969 and 1973. It is a record I am proud of, and one which I believe holds a moral for cricketers of all ability.

6 Man Management

Cricket, I am glad to say, has emerged from the dark ages when a distinction was made between the academic amateur and the professional who relied on the sport for his bread and butter. Such a system encouraged unnecessary internal divisions. Now we are all cricketers working towards the same objective, and man management is recognized as one of the most important jobs facing any captain.

A team is a patchwork of different temperaments and attitudes. Your task as skipper is to be aware of individuals' needs without letting them work against the common good. It is essential to be honest and scrupulously fair with your players. Nothing is more certain to undermine team spirit than judging different players by different rules, as was the case when the amateur influence in cricket was strong. Any team I have captained has been left in no doubt that I have no favourities.

When I joined Leicestershire, for instance, several of the senior members of the playing staff did not seem to regard punctuality as essential. I responded by saying that anyone who failed to turn up on time for any away game would be expected to make his own way to the ground. This led to Brian Davison, the Rhodesian all-rounder, having to make a frantic and expensive dash in a taxi from Leicester to Northampton one morning. I refused to refund his expenses, knowing that younger players would be influenced by the fact that a leading member of the first team was subject to the same code of conduct as them.

It is human nature to react to a man you can trust. That is why I always made a point of telling my players the truth, albeit sometimes diluted in the interests of diplomacy. Brian Luckhurst paid me one of my biggest compliments as a captain during the 1970 Rest of the World series by asking me to give him a realistic appraisal of his chances of making the winter tour of Australia. He told me he would not have asked anyone else, but respected me as a man of integrity who would give him a straight answer. I replied that he was 90 per cent certain of making the trip – which he did – and felt I was working on the right lines with my England team.

Any player under my command must accept criticism and responsibility. If a player does badly I do not want him to start looking for excuses. He should recognize his faults, work on them, and an apology will be gratefully received. Always remember that a captain cannot ask for more than 100 per cent concentration and commitment from his men.

The essence of man management is exploiting the varying natures within your team. These differences in temperament must be recognized, which cannot be done overnight. When I rejoined Yorkshire as manager it took me most of my first season to become familiar with the way individuals needed to be handled, and the manner in which they reacted to given situations.

Some players, like Yorkshire's promising pace bowler Graham Stevenson, respond better to remorseless encouragement. Overzealous criticism could destroy Graham's confidence, and with it his talent. That is not to say, however, that someone like him should be pampered. He must learn to take constructive criticism. In the field a sharp word is a must for anyone who shows signs of allowing his concentration to waver.

Complacency is the captain's biggest enemy, and certainly prevented Leicestershire from enjoying even more success in the John Player League. This became apparent in 1975, the year after we won the League for the first time. Too many players thought it was too easy, with the result that we lost our first four games, and any chance of a realistic challenge. Importantly, we recognized that failing, and in 1976 finished second, level on points with champions Kent, after grasping the need for hard work.

One of the best weapons in the captain's armoury is a clear-the-air meeting, similar to the one I chaired after our disappointing start in 1975. The floor was open to any member of the team, and I acted as mediator to ensure the level of discussion never degenerated into personal abuse. After some frank exchanges of views we came to the general opinion that we had not been trying hard enough in the field on Sundays. Those ideas were worked on, and our results improved. I always encourage my players never to be backward in coming forward with ideas, which I give the greatest thought to before making up my own mind.

It is a good thing for the entire team to consider ways to surmount a particular problem. Another example can be found in the 1978-9 England tour of Australia, where Mike Brearley called a significant team meeting when they were in danger of throwing away the Fourth Test and allowing Australia to square the series. The complacency was banished, Derek Randall scored a magnificent 150, and England retained the Ashes thanks to a superb 93-run win. That was a telling indication of the value of a good team spirit. England strove determinedly towards their ambition and that togetherness was too much for an Australian side who, in the end, betrayed their desperation by bringing in a Rules Football coach to try and motivate them.

One of the features of my time as England captain was the success I had in bringing out the explosive talents of John Snow, cricket's self-styled rebel. 'Snowball' still stands as one of the best examples of my methods of man management.

He was articulate and knew he had been the victim of bad captaincy by being overbowled. But he was also petulant and had what I considered to be a baffling lack of professional pride. He had an infuriating habit of not caring when bad batsmen dealt him needless punishment. Like any new captain, I had to make a lasting initial impact on him. The result was another chapter in a long story of clashes with authority.

In my first Test as captain, against the West Indies at Old Trafford in 1969, Snow was not keen on me making them follow on. It was a decision dictated by unfavourable weather forecasts, and he should have accepted it. I used him sparingly, but wanted him to give me six overs' maximum effort when Basil d'Oliveira made the breakthrough, after Fredericks and Carew had started the second innings by putting on 92 for the first wicket. Snow's reluctance was obvious when he went through the motions, cruising through the spell by bowling strict military medium.

Like the schoolboy thumbing his nose at his headmaster, he needed to be taught a lesson. I insisted he should be left out of the first of three Tests against New Zealand. Snow was not happy, but has since admitted he appreciated me telephoning him soon after the decision was made to explain my reasons. I was playing for Leicestershire at Edgbaston, checked that the chairman of selectors Alec Bedser had been in touch with Snow, and then explained to him I would not tolerate lack of effort. However, I added the important postscript that he would definitely be playing in the Second Test. The whole episode ended with Snow beginning to realize I would back him only if I got his support on the field in return.

Snow still had to be made fully aware of his responsibilities to the rest of the team, and had to be threatened with sending home from the 1970-71 Australian tour before the message sank in. Never the most enthusiastic fielder, he was especially slack in an early game against South Australia. This angered Peter Lever, a wholehearted bowler, and meant I had to act quickly to heal a potentially damaging split in the tour party.

I summoned Snow to manager David Clark's room and reasoned with him as an intelligent man. He saw my argument that if I allowed him to be lackadaisical that lack of concern could infect the rest of the side. I reiterated my intention to use him as my strike bowler, and he repaid me by visibly increasing his work-rate in the field. Like any good captain I thanked Snow for his extra effort. Because of our earlier contretemps Snow knew me as a man of principle. He realized that if he had not reacted in

OPPOSITE *John Snow, a controversial but compelling fast bowler, dismisses Gordon Greenidge*

that way I would have sent him home, even if it had meant losing the Ashes.

Snow, and several of the England team, appreciated that I was concerned with the welfare of my players. At whatever level you play, a captain should make himself available to fight for the rights of his team. A players' captain, who battles for his side against any injustice, wins their trust and respect. That results in total endeavour on the field.

I have been lucky that teams under my command have adopted a sensible, professional attitude. I trusted my players as men and never had to introduce curfews to stop too many late nights. What was made clear was that if I discovered they had been letting me down, they would be punished.

It is no crime for a player to go out with friends for a few beers during a match. Cricket has different demands from a sport like football, where the tension is defused by the 90 minutes hurly burly on a Saturday afternoon. Cricketers are under pressure for days at a time, and need to relax. But moderation in all things is the best policy.

Basil d'Oliveira, that likeable South African-born all-rounder, is one of cricket's great socializers. Before I became England captain he tended to find himself in disciplinary trouble, and there were those who felt he did not have the temperament to withstand the rigours of a long arduous tour.

I had to fight hard to get him included on the Ashes tour of 1970-71, and once I succeeded I wasted no time in impressing upon him the need not to let me down. Basil was the perfect tourist. His sense of humour was a boon to the touring party, and he was a model of dependability. More than a month of the tour had elapsed when he asked for my permission to have a night on the town, and as he was not playing at the time I agreed. Basil enjoyed a typical high-spirited evening, endured the hangover, and was at the ground the next morning to give his moral support to the team.

A tour is the perfect place to build a team spirit which can win matches. Many a side has gone away unrated, but the very fact they are underdogs far away from home cements a bond between the players. If men are determined to work for one another a captain's job is a lot easier.

I am no male chauvinist, but will put myself in the feminists' gunsights by coming out against allowing wives unrestricted access to their cricketing husbands on tour. What is often overlooked is that a female presence can undermine the captain's attempts to build a good team spirit. It might sound heartless, but if there are, say, three wives with the touring party at any one time a captain is not going to have the undivided attention of three players. A far better arrangement would be to have an 'open season' when all wives are allowed on the tour simultaneously.

A captain is always striving to get his team thinking and acting as one man. To reach that goal it is essential the squad mixes together socially as much as possible. Relaxing over a pint or two is the perfect way for the team to get to know one another, discuss problems and means of helping one another.

On that Ashes tour the party made a habit of congregating in my hotel room, where the fridge was stacked with beer and other refreshments. We sang, joked, and talked of professional and patriotic pride.

I stressed to the players what they were representing, and our obligations to live up to the hopes of millions of cricket fans on the other side of the world. Patriotism may be unfashionable in some quarters, but it has a telling impact in international sport. I always remember the awed tones of former Australian wicket-keeper Wally Grout when he said he could almost see the Union Jack billowing behind Ken Barrington as he strode out to bat.

As time went on I could sense we were welding into a formidable unit whose strength was based on our inter-reliance. Team spirit is a nebulous thing that can come out in funny ways. Peter Lever, for instance, always greeted me with his quickest bouncer of the day when I played against him after that tour. He was not being mean, but mischievous, because in our hotel room get-togethers he insisted I could not hook him as well as I had been hooking the Australian bowlers.

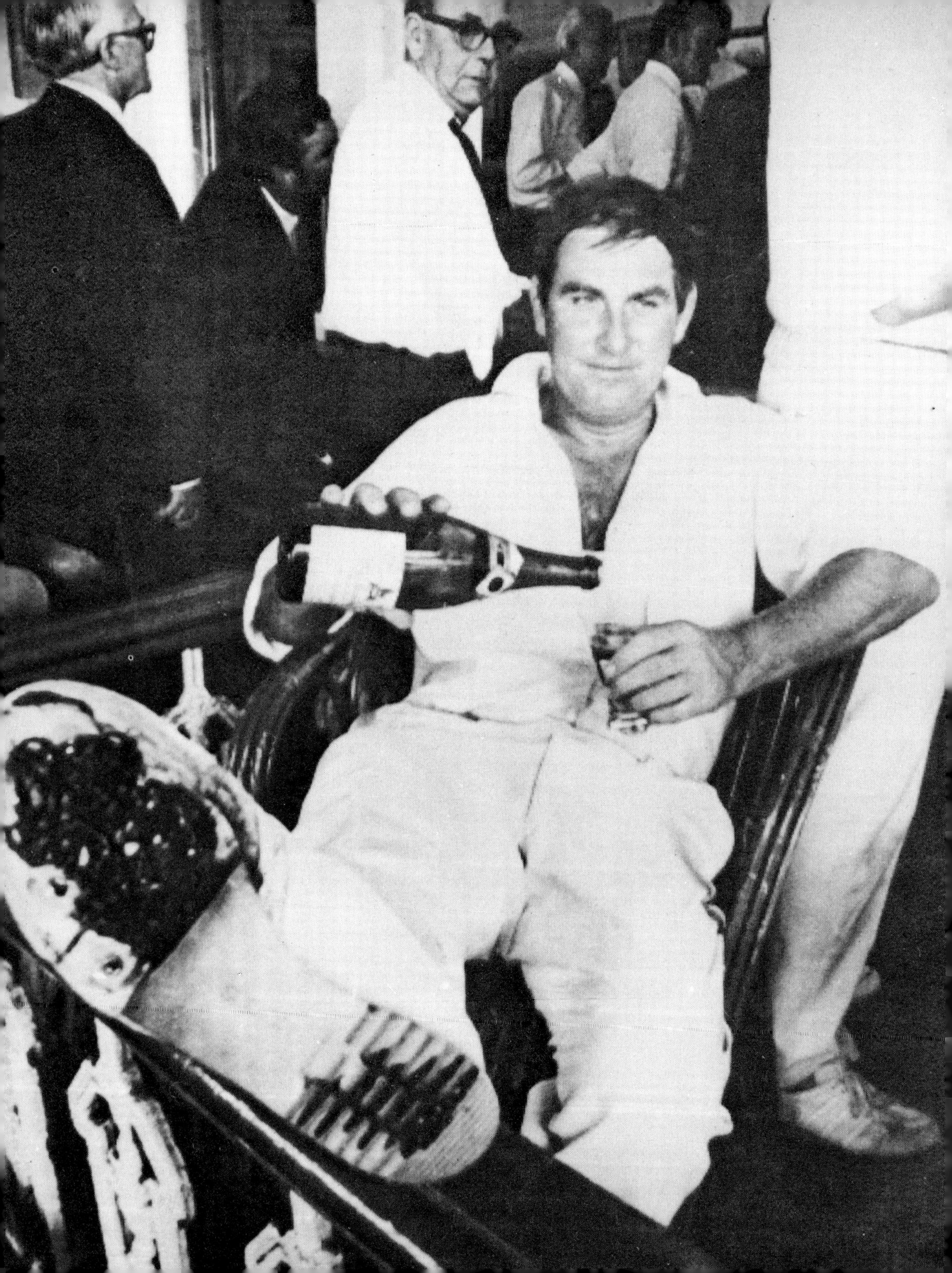

The club captain may think the experiences of an Ashes tour have no relevance to him. But the principles are the same. A team that plays together works well together. Pride, I believe, should be reflected in the way a side dresses. A sloppily dressed team is a lazy team. Leicestershire, for instance, always wore blazers for lunch when I was in charge, and Yorkshire players have to wear a collar and tie for the first two days of any game. Smart casual clothes are allowed for travelling.

These rules are not petty. On the face of it not wearing a blazer may not qualify you for a place in the rogues' gallery. But the blazer is a symbol of your rank as a county cricketer, and you should have pride in that. I find it sad that some counties allow their players to turn up like jumble-sale models. This can only set a bad example to the younger supporters, who regard them as heroes to be emulated.

I regard it as a serious subject, but there is always room for humour. David Gower, untidy in his early days, had an amusing response to my pleas for smartness. Leicestershire had travelled down to Taunton and it seemed just another breakfast in another hotel. But then in came Gower, resplendent in a dinner jacket. The dining room dissolved into helpless laughter and David, having impishly made his point, took mine and smartened himself up.

That is the sort of story that fuels David's image as the happy-go-lucky golden boy of English cricket. It goes without saying he has a great deal of talent, but he would not have reached the top so quickly without his ice-cool temperament. For one so young he has an astonishing maturity.

David is the exception rather than the rule. Captains must nurse young players with the care they lavish on their wives or special girlfriends. Cricket, more than almost any other sport, preys on the nerves of the inexperienced.

The solitary 150-yard walk to the wicket is a purgatory of self-doubt even for the seasoned cricketer. A captain should talk to a young player before he goes in to bat. You can either chat about the way the game is going or discuss something completely

OPPOSITE *The impact of the greatest moment of my captaincy career is beginning to be felt. Champagne tastes better when you have just won the Ashes*

Of all the young players I encountered as a captain, David Gower had the best temperament

different to take his mind off it. I always tell youngsters never to be afraid of talking to themselves in a tense situation. Think positive, whether you are striding out to the crease or waiting under a skied catch.

Young players must be made to feel part of the team from the moment they are introduced, and it is a great help if you take some of the nerves away be reassuring them that they are not on trial. Talent can easily be sabotaged by tension if a player is too aware that one piece of luck could hamper his progress.

That is why I broke with tradition and became the first England captain to ask selectors to give extended chances to certain individuals. When Keith Fletcher and Dennis Amiss, both prone to nerves, began their Test careers under me I told them they were in the side for at least two Tests, which meant the pressure to make an immediate impression was eased a little.

The true test of a young player, or a captain for that matter, is when he is doing badly. The ability to fight your way through a crisis is one of the keys required to open the door to sporting success. There are times when things go wrong through sheer bad luck. In such circumstances sympathy and support are needed. But slackness should be pounced upon. A youngster must be reminded about the worth of practice and the captain must mercilessly criticize his team if their problems are self-inflicted.

It is impossible to overestimate the importance of giving young talent every opportunity to flourish. This is why it is best to appoint a mature, sensible person as captain of the lower sides at club and county level.

We at Yorkshire have just made Colin Johnson, an experienced first-eleven player, second-team captain. Colin is level headed, has a good eye for talent, and will teach youngsters the basics of the game. It is his job to set standards of dress and discipline that will hold good as the promising player climbs the cricket ladder.

Man management, then, is a many-headed creature. But the heart of success in the field lies in the captain's ability to read and use the temperaments of his players. There can be problems, especially in room sharing, where the foibles of each player are magnified.

On England tours, where only the captain and his deputy have single rooms, it has become a tradition to switch players around so they share with as many team-mates as possible. This means the party get to know one another better, and helps avoid the formation of damaging cliques.

However, you have to be careful when supervising the sleeping arrangements of diverse characters such as Geoff Boycott and Alan Knott, who roomed together at the start of the Ashes tour. It was not one of cricket's great partnerships. Geoff likes to lie in, having a lesiurely breakfast sometime after 9 am. Knotty, in contrast, compulsively organizes himself, and needs to rise at 6.30 in order to be ready for breakfast at eight. He is the type of person who sets himself a daily routine that must be followed to the letter: 15 minutes, for instance, is allotted for a shave; 10 minutes for cleaning his teeth and half an hour to get dressed. This regimentation unnerved Geoff, who also lost valuable sleep. They admired each other professionally, but had about as much in common as Paul Raymond and Mary Whitehouse.

My room-mate during my playing days with Yorkshire was Douggie Padgett, who could sleep through an earthquake. I used to get up, have breakfast, and then begin nagging him to get out of bed. We always got on very well, because we were considerate to one another.

I also used to room with Brian Close, but that came to an end when he acquired an obsessive interest in wrestling. I did not take to being rudely awoken at 7.30 am by Closey practising his back hammerlock on me. Brian is one of my most enduring friends in cricket and was best man at my wedding in 1958. But even I never realized he would fancy himself as a second Mick McManus. That just goes to show how hard it is really to know a player....

7 The Pressures of Today

A captain in first-class cricket has to learn to live in the dazzling glare of the spotlight. Countless column inches are devoted to his side in the newspapers, ball-by-ball commentaries are broadcast on the radio, and every decision can be scrutinized by the all-seeing eye of television. The media, whether you like it or not, can influence success or failure.

Even at club level a captain must be aware of the value of the Press. His job is to get as much exposure for the club as possible, and to do that he should forge close links with the cricket reporter on the local paper. He can offer to submit reports, or make himself available to give a detailed rundown of matches and other club topics.

It is important to realize there is more to publicity than satisfying the ego of your players, who love to see their name in print. Remember the sports pages of the local newspaper offer free advertisment for the club. The more impressive the regular coverage of your affairs, the better chance you have of attracting new members.

Higher up the scale every county has its journalistic camp followers. We in Yorkshire have always been accompanied by a large Press contingent consisting of several local reporters and representatives of the national newspapers. It is the responsibility of both captain and journalist to establish a working relationship based on trust.

No other facet of a skipper's job promotes such suspicion, panic and paranoia. Some captains, like Sir Len Hutton and

Geoff Boycott, illustrate their basic insecurity by being frightened of the power of the Press and never trusting a reporter.

This can lead to ridiculous incidents such as the one concerning Len, myself and John Bapty, distinguished former cricket correspondent of the *Yorkshire Evening Post.* We were playing at Bournemouth and after I bowled a tight spell without too much luck John asked me whether the ball was turning. 'A little,' I answered, only to be immediately contradicted by Len. When we were together in the dressing room Hutton told me, 'Never say it is turning when you have not taken wickets.' I had no doubt that Len was trying to act in what he thought were my best interests, but it was petty and needless.

It took any reporter years of personal contact before Len trusted him. In contrast, throughout my career I made a point of initially placing my faith in a journalist's integrity. I was occasionally let down by certain individuals who allowed personal friendships to cloud their objectivity, but I believe I was respected for my actions.

One of the media's current hobby horses is for players to be allowed freedom of speech. I do not disagree with the basic principle, but there must be responsibility on both sides of the sporting fence. It does sport no good when public slanging matches are allowed to develop, but as a captain and now a manager I have rarely refused a reporter access to a player.

I have never been afraid of sensible, constructive criticism. But the Press have to be aware of the impact they can make, especially on a young player. As I have said earlier in this book, it is the captain's duty to protect the more inexperienced lad, and that includes shielding him from the extremes of public comment.

At Yorkshire we have banned any member of the team from commentating on a match that involves the county. This decision stems from our Benson and Hedges semi-final against Essex at Chelmsford last summer when Geoff Boycott, who was unfit to play, apparently criticized his team-mates on television. This did nothing to help morale and angered many members.

Television plays a valuable role in stimulating public interest in sport, but also has its harmful side-effects. None is more damaging than the way it acts as judge and jury over the type of controversial incidents that it relishes highlighting. In my career I twice had cause to rue the manner in which television uses its power.

I was the centre of a storm during the climactic final Test of the 1970-71 tour of Australia at Sydney, where I led the team off the field. That was necessary after angry crowd scenes related to another incident, where I clashed with umpire Lou Rowan.

He warned Snow for intimidatory bowling after Terry Jenner ducked into a short ball, and pictures depicting me angrily wagging a finger at the umpire were flashed around the world. Taken at face value those pictures, which were used prominently on television news, showed me fragrantly flouting the umpire's authority. This was a wholly mistaken view. In fact, instead of admonishing Rowan I was reminding him, albeit forcibly, that Snow had bowled just one bouncer. I asked him under what rule the warning was issued. The media did not bother to contact me for my version of the incident, and were too quick to condemn me for a crime I did not commit.

The second furore stoked by television came later in the summer of 1971, when Snow barged Sunny Gavaskar to the ground during the Lord's Test. It was an indefensible action, but blown out of all proportion. Television delighted in constantly screening slow-motion replays of the incident, and virtually forced the authorities to take some kind of action.

Gavaskar accepted it was a heat of the moment lapse on Snow's part, and was satisfied by his apologies. They had a drink together and as England captain I was prepared to let the whole thing rest. However, television acted like a dog with a juicy bone and refused to stop chewing the matter over until disciplinary action was taken.

Like any captain worth his salt I tell my players to accept an umpire's decision. I agree that a skipper should set a good example both on and off the field. He and his team have a

responsibility to the cricket public.

I am all for captains playing an integral part in helping county clubs build stronger links with their supporters. The fans who pay the money should not be forgotten the second the season ends. They should be catered for during the winter, and it is good for a captain's duties to include attending member's evenings and the like.

Public speaking is one of the chores of life as a cricket captain. I set a limit on the amount of cricket club dinners I attend because I value my home life, but speak at several functions in an attempt to keep my finger on the pulse of local thinking. Supporters need to realize that professional sportsmen need their private life. It is difficult to cope with the strain of being constantly recognized and pestered. No one needs reminding that such pressures caused the wayward genius of George Best to be lost to soccer.

When I go out socially I am always prepared to answer sensible questions from any member of the public. At heart I still have the same boyish enthusiasm for cricket that led my grandfather to chuckle that I would give my last tuppence to Len Hutton's testimonial fund. But unfortunately there are always ignorant individuals who, usually with the 'wisdom' a bellyful of beer brings, alcoholically regale you about your supposed shortcomings. I feel that is unforgivably bad manners.

That said, I take pains never to snub a well-meaning person and try whenever practical to accede to the pleas for my autograph. Youngsters, though, can try and take advantage of your goodwill. Make no mistake, I know the trials and tribulations of autograph hunting – it took me literally years to get Len Hutton's signature, and I only succeeded when he was watching Pudsey as he recovered from an attack of mumps – but the youngsters of today are not satisfied with just one autograph. You sign their books and they go to the back of the queue to get you to sign again. Such greed erodes anyone's patience.

A top cricketer is an instantly recognizable character in these days of commerciality, when players are used to help sell every-

OPPOSITE *A momentous collision. John Snow sends Sunny Gavaskar crashing to the gound at Lord's in 1971*

thing from cars to cricket bats. A captain should be involved in commercial dealings that benefit his side, but has to know when to draw the line.

In the past cricketers have been exploited with lamentable ease. One of the crucial repercussions of the Packer earthquake was that leading players realized their value. I had already gained a reputation for fighting for what I believed my players deserved, but since then have been disturbed by the signs of money madness creeping in.

Mike Brearley's England squad wanted a pay rise before embarking upon the 1979-80 tour of Australia. When it was refused they did not carry out their muttered threats of withdrawal, which dogged the earlier negotiations. I was thankful for that, but the very fact that cash was apparently considered before the honour of representing England is worrying.

I am not saying a player should allow himself to be financially walked over. By all means accept the lucrative contracts firms are now offering. But the England squad must realize how lucky they are, and that commercial considerations must never divert them from their search for success on the field.

Agents are useful in that they have a better idea of a player's market value. But the captain is still a valuable source of information regarding contracts. I always advised younger members of the staff to look closely at the terms offered, and made myself available to answer any queries.

That sort of close relationship was unheard of when I entered the first-class game in 1951. The traditional captain was an aloof amateur who changed in a different room and even stayed in a different hotel. Many things have altered since then, and each step forward has brought extra pressure.

The ever-increasing influence of one-day cricket is linked to most of the additional strains. Travelling, for instance, is a burden disliked by most county cricketers. The thought of travelling the length and breadth of the country to play cricket may seem glamorous and exciting to the schoolboy behind the boundary rail. But in real life slogging away down motorways and main

OPPOSITE *Sir Len Hutton, my boyhood idol*

roads saps enthusiasm and breeds boredom. Four hours or more in a car is no way for a professional sportsman to prepare for an important match.

When my first-class career began, one-day cricket was not even a twinkle in the sponsors' eye. We played two three-day games a week, and generally travelled on Tuesday and Friday evenings. Now, with the John Player League making county cricket a seven-day proposition, you can make three trips in a weekend. Teams are all too often expected to travel to a venue for a Championship match which starts on Saturday, leave for another Sunday League fixture, and then return to continue the three-day game. This involves hundreds of miles. Surely it is possible to play the game in different competitions on Saturday and Sunday?

Limited-overs cricket has, of course, had a fundamental influence. I have already discussed the way its negative aims of containment have seeped into all spheres of the game. A captain is under enormous pressure for shorter periods of time. If he makes a slight error of judgement in a three-day match he has time to paper over the cracks and recover from it. In the more instant environment of one-day cricket a single mistake is usually enough to invite defeat.

A club captain, with the mushrooming of the League system in this country, is subject to the same demands as a county captain. There may not be quite the strain of being in the public eye, but he has to balance efficiency with harmony. Almost every club side has its weaker members whose enthusiasm outweighs their ability but they may become disenchanted if not regularly asked to bat or bowl.

I do not agree with the theory that the cash injected into cricket by the new breed of sponsors adds to the pressure on a captain and his men. Players would not be human if they did not consider the financial implications of success, but they place more importance on winning a major honour for the glory. A healthy bank balance is no great consolation for a career bereft of the supreme thrill of winning medals.

A captain is more of an administrative figure than before, and that trend gives us the clearest indication of the future. I envisage the skipper assuming the role of right-hand man to a county manager. My experience as Yorkshire manager, and the practicality of my liaison with captain John Hampshire, has convinced me that this is one great way for cricket to progress.

As I said in my introduction, a captain has been expected to be the jack of all trades and master of some. His influence will be just as significant if he is given time to concentrate on cricket matters by the appointment of a manager. Certainly Geoff Boycott, an intense individual, would have been more likely to be a successful captain had the niggling chores of the job been taken away by someone with the brief I now hold.

John has been left free to devote the majority of his time to cricket matters. I, as manager, deal with Press relations, travel arrangements, ticket queries and the myriad other mundane things that crop up. Even an England captain is bedevilled by petty administration that often takes an hour which should be used in considered preparation.

A manager would have been the answer to my prayers on the Saturday of the Second Test against the West Indies at Edgbaston in 1973. I arrived at the ground at 10 am to be greeted by a totally unexpected crisis: umpire Arthur Fagg was refusing to stand as a result of a row with Rohan Kanhai. The next 90 minutes were spent in a series of meetings with Fagg and frantic periods on the telephone trying to contact someone in authority. When play started I hadn't even changed into my whites, but Fagg was finally persuaded to make his protest through official channels. Of course, everyone in the ground wanted me to forget those traumas and act like a cricketing version of Confucius....

8 Captains I Have Known

BRIAN CLOSE (YORKSHIRE, SOMERSET AND ENGLAND)

Strengths

In his element leading from the front. He relished attacking situations, encouraging his spinners and never hesitating to field in suicidal positions. An unselfish man whose infectious enthusiasm is a vastly underestimated influence in Somerset's success. Only Richie Benaud was a better captain.

Weaknesses

An impulsive personality who needed a challenge to occupy his fertile brain. Tended to lose concentration during lulls in play, when Yorkshire wicketkeeper Jimmy Binks would whisper to me, 'Eh up Illy, t'rudder's gone again.' It was my job, as right-hand man, to snap Brian out of the day-dreaming.

OPPOSITE *No one could set a more courageous example to a team than Brian Close, seen here being hit on the chest by a Michael Holding bouncer*

RONNIE BURNET (YORKSHIRE)

Strengths

Ronnie revitalized a somewhat disenchanted Yorkshire team with his honesty and total commitment. Had the strength of character to deal with any troublemaker, but was humble enough to accept his technical shortcomings. Although proud of his position, he never felt it was beneath him to pick the brains of others. Tenacious and trustworthy, he excelled in his handling of young players.

Weaknesses

Superfically he typified the type who unfortunately dominated captaincy before the war. An amateur, he was in no way worth his place on playing ability. A mediocre batsman, he had to be hidden in the field. His grasp of tactics was not overwhelmingly impressive.

GEOFF BOYCOTT (YORKSHIRE AND ENGLAND)

Strengths

Technically still the outstanding candidate to captain England. Reads the game well and is not afraid of decisions. Earlier in his career he could literally read my mind. I intended to ask what end I should bowl during the Edgbaston Test against West Indies in 1973, but before I had a chance to speak he told me both my question and his answer. If Colin Cowdrey had refused the vice-captaincy of the 1970-71 Ashes tour, I would have wanted Geoff as my deputy. That could have changed the face of recent Test history.

Weaknesses

A tragic victim of his own temperament. Far too intense, Geoff finds it difficult to mix with other players and allows the personal struggle for batting perfection to dominate his life. Unable to grasp that patience is needed with young players. He came into the Yorkshire side when Fred Trueman and I were at the peak of our powers, and expects his inexperienced youngsters to reach the same standard.

OPPOSITE *Geoff Boycott, whose intense personality prevented a successful career as England captain*

NORMAN YARDLEY (YORKSHIRE AND ENGLAND)

Strengths

Possessed a comprehensive tactical knowledge and was able to maintain a high level of concentration. An instantly likeable man, Norman was impeccably qualified for the job, being a middle-order batsman who complemented his usefulness as a medium pacer by being a brave close fielder.

Weaknesses

Would be recognized as one of England's best post-war skippers but for one endearingly human failing: he was too nice. That flaw led to his authority being flouted by some of the more overpowering characters under his command. Many times Norman would ask me to bowl, and take no action when someone like Bob Appleyard refused to come off in my favour. This naturally upset me and damaged team spirit.

SIR LEN HUTTON (YORKSHIRE AND ENGLAND)

Strengths

My boyhood idol, he commanded respect because of his brilliance as a batsman. His own experience as a player made him a fine reader of batsmen. In my early days he exploited Tom Graveney's temperamental failings by putting me on with instructions to bowl tightly. He knew I would frustrate him into submission.

Weaknesses

Painfully uncomfortable in company, he was too much of a loner. Did not even stay in the same hotel as his team. One of the biggest culprits of time wasting in Test cricket – he thought nothing of walking 40 yards to tell Frank Tyson to take his time – Len was too conscious of the impact of fast bowlers. Tended to underemploy spinners.

COLIN COWDREY (KENT AND ENGLAND)

Strengths

A complex character who had a strong sense of public relations. His manners were impeccable, and he could be a thoughtful, kind man to players he favoured. Blessed with immense natural talent which he did not use as effectively as someone like May.

Weaknesses

Found it impossible to make split-second decisions, betraying a basic lack of security by asking too many people for their opinion. Rarely built warm, lasting relationships with his team because of a tendency to have favourites. Condemned to ultimate failure as a captain through essentially being an amateur trying to make himself a professional.

TONY GREIG (SUSSEX AND ENGLAND)

Strengths

One of the most imposing and influential captains in the history of English cricket. The true gauge of his charismatic personality was the great spirit he instilled into a side that tasted failure before success. Anyone can foster good morale in a winning team. Greig revelled in the pressure-cooker atmosphere of top sport, and it was typical that many of his greatest triumphs were moulded out of adversity. His seven-hour century in the 1977 Calcutta Test against India, when he batted with a temperature of 104, was characteristic. Players respond to that kind of selfless determination.

Weaknesses

The extrovert image, fuelled by quick-fire quotes, overshadowed technical deficiencies. There have been many better readers of a game. His downfall came from the realization of his commercial aspirations. I did not blame anyone for joining Packer, but Greig used the exalted position of England captain to canvass for WSC. Now head of a thriving insurance firm in Australia, he may live in palatial splendour and have an enviable bank balance, but I suspect he would pay heavily to turn the clock back and captain England again.

3 NEW

MIKE BREARLEY (MIDDLESEX AND ENGLAND)

Strengths

The statistics suggest he is one of the greatest England captains. The luckiest would be more the truth. He has enjoyed lucrative success against sub-standard Test teams. That said, he has shown that his time studying the sub-conscious areas of psychology was not wasted. Has the respect and trust of his players, and showed in his early days at Middlesex that he would not tolerate any cliques in his side. So do not be fooled by the educated facade. He is a shrewd, ruthless leader.

Weaknesses

There can be little argument that he is not a Test class batsman. Technical failings have been constantly exposed, but he has survived because the team is successful. It is significant the cracks showed during his first real test, against the polished West Indies, in the 1979 World Cup final. Brearley made basic tactical mistakes in the handling of his bowlers, should have dropped himself down the order and promoted a natural strokeplayer like David Gower to open with Boycott.

Mike Brearley celebrates a Test win in time honoured style – with a drink

PETER MAY (SURREY AND ENGLAND)

Strengths

The archetypal amateur with a professional's outlook, Peter played his cricket hard without losing his natural dignity. Treated his players as equals, whatever their experience. In return received unswerving loyalty. May, the batsman, deserves that overworked adjective, great. Technically close to perfection, he was a merciless destroyer of the best attacks.

Weaknesses

Slightly stereotyped tactically, predictable and hesitant to take risks. This could have been because of his over-sensitivity to criticism. I believe Press comments on his ability as captain hastened his retirement.

MIKE SMITH (WARWICKSHIRE AND ENGLAND)

Strengths

Pleasant personality who instilled a great sense of purpose into his teams. Ready to praise, but tempered that by not being afraid to criticize. His unorthodox batting style made him a destroyer of mediocre spin or seam bowling, but was transparently vulnerable to an early yorker. Technically sound, with a reputation for setting fair declarations.

Weaknesses

His major fault can probably be put down to the county he played for. Warwickshire have a woeful record of producing good spinners, and consequently Smith had no real idea when to use their specialist talent.

OPPOSITE LEFT *Peter May, a classical batsman and captain who demanded respect*

RIGHT *Mike Smith*

MICKY STEWART (SURREY AND ENGLAND)

Strengths

The talent neglected by England is now being successfully exploited by Surrey, revitalized under his management. An honest man who commands great respect, and his basic understanding of the game is easily transmitted to young players. Micky knows when to sympathize and when to slate, and I was surprised he was never given the opportunity to lead his country during the mid-1960s.

Weaknesses

During crucial times in his career he was dogged by suggestions he was not quite good enough as a batsman for England. Although his love of hooking was punished, he moved his feet well and was a better player than Brearley.

STUART SURRIDGE (SURREY AND ENGLAND)

Strengths

A bright breezy optimist, Stuart was a born leader. His confidence was as contagious as radioactivity, and he became a master of the inspired gamble. Of course, he had one of the strongest county attacks ever assembled under his command. But such was the enthusiasm he engendered he might have been successful with a bunch of short-sighted old-age pensioners.

Weaknesses

Surprisingly few for an amateur. He could not match the extremely high standards of Alec Bedser, Loader, Laker and Lock, but was a capable medium pacer. Brave close to the bat, he was not a good fielder in the deep.

OPPOSITE *Two fine Surrey captains: Micky Stewart (left) with Stuart Surridge*

TED DEXTER (SUSSEX AND ENGLAND)

Strengths

A man of moods whose ability as a captain was only apparent in the instant environment of one-day cricket. Tactically aggressive, he understood cricket well. Similarly, as a batsman thrived when the pressure was on.

Weaknesses

Anyone who saw 'Lord Ted' idly practising his golf swing at third man knew his total unsuitability for captaincy. His concentration was poor, and be became bored too quickly. Instigated one of the longest drinks breaks in cricket when he ordered the Sussex twelfth man to smuggle a radio on to the pitch so he could listen to the Derby. Play did not re-start until he had heard the commentary. So vague his wife asked me once, 'Has he spoken to you today? When I said no, she replied: 'Oh good, it is not me then....'

MIKE DENNESS (KENT, ESSEX AND ENGLAND)

Strengths

Mike had the misfortune to be appointed England captain too early in his career. Since leaving Kent has become more relaxed and better suited to the demands of the job. A solid batsman, rarely spectacular but more reliable than, say, Mike Brearley.

Weaknesses

Being pitched in against West Indies and an Australian side featuring the twin terrors of Lillee and Thomson highlighted his failings. He did not have the strength of character to pull round his battered and bruised England team, and fell into the trap of being too distant from his players. However, I must emphasize the unfortunate timing of his appointment.

EDDIE BARLOW (DERBYSHIRE AND SOUTH AFRICA)

Strengths

The Billy Bunter figure of Barlow is proof of the power of positive thinking. His policy as a player or captain is unchanging: attack whenever possible. That sort of attitude transformed Derbyshire from a group of dispirited individuals into a slick, confident team. He stressed the importance of physical fitness, and bowlers threw off their inferiority complex because of Barlow's constant encouragement.

Weaknesses

Could be made to pay for his attacking intentions. As a bowler he was punished for pitching the ball up, and, as a batsman who looked to play his strokes, was vulnerable to the ball that nipped back into him. Was prepared to order his men to make positive attempts for victory, which sometimes led to desperate rearguard actions.

MIKE PROCTER (GLOUCESTERSHIRE AND SOUTH AFRICA)

Strengths

The ideal subject if you had to explain the meaning of leading by example to a visitor from Mars. Fiery new-ball bowler and adequate off-spinner, he bats with savage grace and power. His philosophy is very much like fellow countryman Barlow – defence is only assumed if imperative.

Weaknesses

The inherent danger with such a fine all-round player is that he will begin to believe the chants of 'Proctershire'. At the moment his team needs him, but if they develop young players he may have to ease up on his role to facilitate their progress. As a batsman he is surprisingly unhappy against pace and can be reduced to rash aggression by an accurate spinner.

SIR GARY SOBERS (NOTTINGHAMSHIRE AND WEST INDIES)

Strengths

The greatest all-round player the world has ever seen, he was happy to stand or fall by his belief that cricket, even at Test level, should be entertaining. He took risks, and was unfairly criticized for them, especially when his sporting declaration cost the West Indies the Fourth Test at Port of Spain in 1968. Calculating his only chance of victory was to give England an accessible target, he asked them to make 215 in 165 minutes. Despite some inititial hesitation by Cowdrey, England succeeded. The critics had a field day, but Gary never lost the support of his players.

Weaknesses

Took too much on when he was hailed as the Messiah of Nottinghamshire. One of my most profitable wagers involved betting he would never do the double in county cricket. Gary did not have the concentration and tended to become embroiled in horse racing, his other passion. He unwittingly ruined one match against Leicestershire by studying form, forgetting that he had to declare until it was too late.

ROHAN KANHAI (WARWICKSHIRE AND WEST INDIES)

Strengths

Tactically astute captain who made few mistakes because of his wealth of experience. A dedicated batsman who expected the same from his players.

Weaknesses

A loner who alienated his players, especially the younger ones, by criticizing rather than encouraging. People became frightened of making mistakes under him, and his lack of popularity was reflected in some surprising results. For instance a team with any sort of spirit would not have allowed a patently outclassed England to draw the 1974-75 series in the West Indies.

INTIKHAB ALAM (SURREY AND PAKISTAN)

Strengths

Like India, Pakistan do not help themselves by changing their captain with frantic regularity. Some typically thoughtful manipulation of his players by Inti made a nonsense of the lack of job security. A gentle likeable man, better suited than a garrulous extrovert to get the best out of his countrymen.

Weaknesses

His introverted nature made him a little retiring in public. Although a superb leg-spinner, he would be more dangerous if he spun the ball more. Not suited to the low, slow Oval wickets, and would have made a bigger impact playing for a county like Nottinghamshire where conditions are kinder.

AJIT WADEKAR (INDIA)

Strengths

Like all Indian captains he placed his faith in the Oriental virtue of patience. A tenacious fighter, and India have much to thank him for. A national hero when he made excellent use of his limited resources to defeat both West Indies and England, but was literally too ashamed to go home immediately after the 3-0 defeat here in 1974, which signalled the end of his career.

Weaknesses

Not the type of personality of which legends are made. Containment, rather than aggression, was his style and it did not make for riveting cricket. When the opportunities were there for attack he found it difficult to shake off his tactical lethargy.

OPPOSITE *Captaincy can be a cruel business. Ajit Wadekar (in blazer) acknowledges the cheers of the crowd after leading India to their historic win over England in the 1971 series. Yet three years later he feared returning home after suffering a 3–0 defeat here*

BEV CONGDON (NEW ZEALAND)

Strengths

A brave battler in the mould of Eddie Barlow, he was the sort of person you would send on a virtually impossible mission in wartime. A stubborn, affable man who exuded professionalism, he instilled his fighting qualities into his New Zealand team. The perfect testament to his determination was his 176 in the Nottingham Test of 1973, which helped them to within 40 runs of overhauling my victory target of 479.

Weaknesses

Being used to playing with his back against the wall, he lacked experience of attacking situations. Ambition has never been a characteristic of Kiwi captains.

BOBBY SIMPSON (AUSTRALIA)

Strengths

A typical product of the Old School, he had the principles needed to keep Australia afloat in the aftermath of the Packer tidal wave. A keen disciplinarian, he demanded professionalism on and off the field. Dedication was apparent from the start, when he became the first Australian to play off-spin effectively. This was through diligent work on his technique, and he eagerly taught it to team-mates.

Weaknesses

Some felt that at times he was out of touch with the untried generation of Aussie cricketers. It might be true to say one or two resented his insistence on a strict code of conduct.

Bevan Congdon – an immensely influential New Zealand captain

BILL LAWRY (AUSTRALIA)

Strengths

More willing to give up his wife than his wicket. A compulsive competitor prepared to fight for any lost cause. At times infuriatingly dull and dour in his tactics – but if you became too rash he delighted in taking advantage.

Weaknesses

Made basic errors in his handling of bowlers. John Gleeson, for instance, was used as a stock bowler instead of being recognized as potentially his most valuable weapon. Many England batsman during the Ashes tour of 1970-71 were in dreadful trouble against him but escaped because Lawry did not have the imagination to post close fielders for the inevitable bat-pad chances. All-out attack was anathema to him.

IAN CHAPPELL (AUSTRALIA)

Strengths

Brash, bullheaded but always positive, Ian would have made a good county captain. He fought hard, although tactlessly, for his players, and in return received respect and unswerving loyalty. A good reader of a game, he never gave less than 100 per cent.

Weaknesses

Very much the Jekyll and Hyde character of world cricket. After we won the Ashes in Australia he seemed to overcompensate for the lack of hardness in the team. This led to the slovenly, surly squad he was in charge of until 1975. Captaincy did not reduce his effectiveness as a batsman, although he had an initial weakness with the hook.

OPPOSITE *Ian Chappell: argumentative but a good captain*

RICHIE BENAUD (AUSTRALIA)

Strengths

A fitting man with whom to end the book. The nearest thing we are ever going to get to the perfect cricket captain. He matched boyish enthusiasm with ceaseless concentration, calculated attack and non-stop encouragement. He knew what made people tick, almost demanding that his bowlers should take wickets. The standard sermon was: 'C'mon Illy, you can do this fellow. I'll give you a couple of short legs.' After a while you would be so convinced of your talent you would be prepared to put your life savings on capturing wickets.

Richie is still the complete professional, and uses the qualities he developed as a captain in television commentating. Just as he treated young players with care and respect, so he helps the occasional broadcaster – like me – by always giving prior warning if he requires your views.

Weaknesses

None. If you do not believe that you have not met Benaud. I guarantee: half an hour with him and he could persuade you to sell your grandmother.